LOUIS MAJORELLE

Master of Art Nouveau design

Louis Majorelle

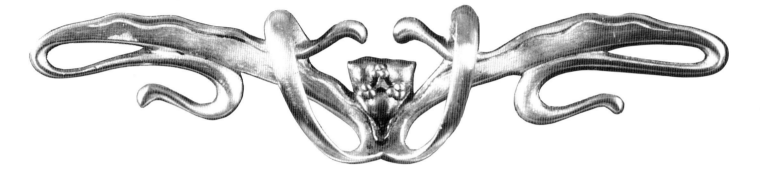

Master of Art Nouveau design

ALASTAIR DUNCAN

FOREWORD BY LLOYD MACKLOWE
AND BARBARA MACKLOWE

Harry N. Abrams, Inc., Publishers, New York

Half-title-page illustration: cover of a Majorelle sales catalogue
Title-page illustration: a gilt-bronze handle from a
dressing-table drawer.

LIBRARY OF CONGRESS CATALOGING-IN-PUBLICATION DATA
Duncan, Alastair.
Louis Majorelle : master of art nouveau design / Alastair Duncan:
foreword by Lloyd Macklowe and Barbara Macklowe.
p. cm.
Includes bibliographical references and index.
ISBN 0–8109–3617–8
1. Majorelle, Louis. 1859–1926—Criticism and interpretation.
2. Decoration and ornament—France—Art nouveau. 3. Decoration and
ornament—France—History—19th century. I. Title.
NK1535.M24D8 1991
745.4'492—dc20   91–11996

Contents

Acknowledgments

Grateful thanks are extended to the many individuals and institutions, whose generous assistance in providing information and photographs has made possible the compilation of this book:

Claudia Asper (Christie's Geneva); M. Barbier-Ludwig (Musée de l'Ecole de Nancy); Georges de Bartha (Hapsburg-Feldman S.A.); Nico Borsje; Frederick Brandt (Virginia Museum of Fine Arts, Richmond, Virginia); Jean-Claude Brugnot; Judy Bush and Jessica Rutherford (Brighton Art Gallery and Museum, Sussex); Gary and Janet Calderwood; M. Carton (Archives Départementales de Meurthe-et-Moselle, Nancy); Mark Clark and Irene Roughton (Chrysler Museum, Norfolk, Virginia); Jane Farmer; Barry Friedman; Philippe Garner (Sotheby's, London); Burt and Paula Geyer; Thomas D. Grischkowksy (The Museum of Modern Art, New York); Henry Hawley (The Cleveland Museum of Art, Cleveland, Ohio); Mr and Mrs Robert Kogod; Mike Larkin (Victoria and Albert Museum, London); Lloyd and Barbara Macklowe; Steve and Dotty Malinchoc; Félix Marcilhac; John and Katsy Mecom, Jr.; R. Craig Miller; Isso Miura; Ferdinand Neess and Anne-Marie; Evelyne Possémé, Suzanne Tise and Sonia Edard (Musée des Arts Décoratifs, Paris); Mme Renson-Le Bris (Archives Municipales de Nancy); Benedict Silverman; Mark Slotkin; Mr and Mrs Jack Stievelman; Norlene Tips; H. J. Van Bel; Guy Vancel, Mlle Marie-Claire Mangin and Mme Marcelle Moret (Bibliothèque Municipale, Nancy); Andrée Vyncke.

Special thanks are due to Mlle Marie-Claire Mangin for her generous help with archival material in the Bibliothèque Municipale, Nancy, and to MaryBeth McCaffrey for her research work and assistance in co-ordinating the entire project.

Photographic credits
The author is indebted to the following for their photographic contributions: Jean-Loup Charmet; Garlich Flörke; Peter Greenhalf; Philippe Husson; Barry Hyman; Earl Lewis; Gilbert Mangin; Alain Melchior (Studio Image, Nancy); David Robinson; Townsend Photo; Karen Willis; and Peter Willy. Sources of individual illustrations are listed below:

Antiquarian Traders, Los Angeles (photos Earl Lewis); pls. 34–36, 43, 79; Courtesy, Georges de Bartha, Hapsburg-Feldman S.A.: pl. 103; Nico Borsje Collection, Paris: *pp. 101 top, 123 bottom centre*; (photos Peter Willy) pls. 50, 117; Butterfield & Butterfield, San Francisco: *p. 100 top left and bottom*; Calderwood Gallery, Philadelphia (photos David Robinson): *pp. 44 right, 104 bottom right, 107 top left, 154 bottom; 157 left and right*; pls. 11, 23, 24, 40, 42, 64, 70, 74, 75, 96; Courtesy, Jean-Pierre Camard: pl. 118; Chasen-Stamati Gallery, New York (photo David Robinson): *p. 110 top left*; Christie's, Geneva: pl. 57; Christie's, New York: *p. 111 bottom right*; pl. 92; Chrysler Museum, Norfolk, Va: *pp. 44 left, 99 bottom left, 103 top left, 105 bottom centre*; pls. 12, 16, 26, 27; Cleveland Museum of Art, Cleveland, Ohio: (Purchase, James Parmelee Fund), *p. 109 centre left*; (John L. Severance Fund 76.53), pl. 33; Editions Denoël, Paris: *pp. 146 top right, 160*; Barry Friedman Ltd, New York: *pp. 102 bottom right, 103 bottom right*; pls. 44, 52, 54, 55, 83, 85; Mr and Mrs Gillion-Crowet: *p. 38*; pl. 134; Homeculture Ltd, Toronto: pls. 41, 45; Philippe Husson: *p. 27*; Macklowe Gallery, New York: *pp. 103 top right, 104 bottom left and centre*; pls. 15, 49, 51, 87, 89, 90, 116, 124, 136; (photo Barry Hyman) pl. 112; (photos Sotheby's, New York) pls. 105–7, 131, 132, 135; Gilbert Mangin, Nancy: *pp. 26, 29 top left*; pls. 1, 2, 104; Félix Marcilhac, Paris: *pp. 104 top left, 115 centre, 123 top centre*; pl. 88; Mr and Mrs John W. Mecom, Jr: (photos David Robinson) *pp. 102 bottom left, 104 top right, 109 top left*; pls. 18, 28, 29, 39, 58, 95, 115; (photo courtesy, Museum of Fine Arts, Houston, Texas) pl. 80; Metropolitan Museum of Art, New York: (Gift of the Sydney and Frances Lewis Foundation, 1979) *p. 100 top right*; (Friends of Twentieth Century Decorative Arts Gift, 1983) *p. 147 top centre*; Courtesy, Isso Miura: pls. 120, 128; Musée des Arts Décoratifs, Paris: pl. 84; Musée des Beaux-Arts, Nancy (photos Gilbert Mangin): pls. 123, 129, 130; Musée de l'Ecole de Nancy: (photos Gilbert Mangin) pls. 56, 114; (photos Studio Image) *p. 149*; pls. 63, 111, 127; Musée d'Orsay, Paris: *p. 105 centre right*; pls. 17, 48, 66; Ferdinand Neess Collection (photos Garlich Flörke): pls. 19, 61, 65, 108, 110; Photo Réalités, Paris: pl. 122; Private Collection (photos David Robinson): pls. 3–5, 46, 60, 62, 67–69, 71, 78, 81, 82, 86, 97, 98, 121; Private Collection (photos Studio Image, Nancy): pls. 93, 94; Joel Schur Collection: *p. 39*; Sotheby's, London and Monaco (photos courtesy, Philippe Garner): *pp. 12, 40 right, 51, 99 top left, 101 below, 102 top right, 105 bottom right, 114 top left and bottom right, 127 bottom left*; pls. 20–22, 32, 37, 38, 47, 53, 59, 72, 73, 76, 113, 126, 133; Sotheby's, New York: *pp. 114 top right, 115 left, 127 bottom left*; pl. 109; Jack and Harriet Stievelman Collection (photos Barry Hyman): pls. 119, 125; Studio Image, Nancy: pls. 6–10, 30, 31, 99–102; Victoria and Albert Museum, London: pls. 13, 14; Virginia Museum of Fine Arts, Richmond, Va: *p. 36*; (Sydney and Frances Lewis Collection) pl. 77; Andrée Vyncke: *pp. 37, 40 left*.

Foreword

AT LAST a book has been written which illuminates the life and works of the great French Art Nouveau designer and furniture maker, Louis Majorelle. Alastair Duncan has drawn on all the available information written on the subject that has survived both a massive fire in 1916 and World War I bombings to produce this book brimming with exquisite photographs.

In the late 1960s, when we made a decision to concentrate our efforts on buying and selling decorative arts of the early twentieth century, we found such a paucity of written material that it was virtually impossible to glean any information except through period publications such as the *International Studio, Art et décoration* and *L'Art décoratif.* At the time the only available book which referred to the School of Nancy was Ada Pollack's *Modern Glass*, which included a few illustrations of French cameo glass with references to museum collections. In 1973, however, a superb catalogue was published in Germany by the Landesmuseum Hessen, Darmstadt, to accompany an exhibition held there, and a few years later Robert Schmutzler's book *Art Nouveau* (translated from the earlier German edition) was published in America; but these were nothing more than *hors d'oeuvres*, trifles to tantalize, with little in-depth information about the furniture and glassmaking of Paris and Nancy.

We have always shared Alastair Duncan's passion for Majorelle furniture and designs. Our interest in Majorelle furniture began as we were strolling down the Marché Paul Bert in the Paris flea market, where we saw a set of decorative panels by Alphonse Mucha of the *Four Seasons* framed within a four-part wooden screen intricately carved with clematis tendrils and blossoms. The year was 1968. The screen was by Louis Majorelle. The price was the equivalent of $400. Although we were smitten, we could not afford it at that time. This story does, fortunately, have a happy ending. We, who had until then been enamoured solely of art glass and Tiffany lamps, now had our eyes opened to the world of Art Nouveau furniture and graphic works, and this gave rise to a consuming interest which eventually led us to open the Macklowe Gallery on Madison Avenue in New York in the fall of 1970.

To transcend all aspects of nature and to recreate its forms while staying within an artistic framework was the creative desire of the turn-of-the-century designers. Few could equal Louis Majorelle in the difficult task of incorporating these natural forms into furniture, light-fixtures and other related media. He showed the flair and exuberance not only of a master cabinetmaker, but also of an artist. He was innovative in his use of rare and opulent woods, both imported and domestic, using this medium as a means to express his visions of nature. Majorelle's forte was a constant awareness of the functionalism of the items he produced, doing so in the vernacular of a fine artist – with originality and beauty of form.

In Majorelle's work the strength and vulnerability of the evolutionary process is often portrayed by a flower, tree or fern. The natural growth pattern is depicted in his carvings and marquetry designs, but is not always botanical in concept, being more poetic and spiritual in its intent, and, as with all living things, evokes a metaphor for life itself.

We feel that, both as collectors and as retail sellers, we are inevitably only temporary custodians of the items we possess. Although our possession may be temporary, many pieces will remain in our mind's eye forever, for some of these have been the stars of our personal collection at home, while others were acquired by us to be sold in our gallery. One such piece acquired for our collection is the rare Majorelle three-branch water-lily lamp, cast in bronze. Its three shades are blossoms of blown or carved art glass in brilliant pink, cushioned by pale-green foliage, produced for Majorelle by Daum Frères of Nancy. The first time we encountered this lamp, with its foot or base forming a lyrical 'swirl' of water-lily stems (colour plate 132) 80cm (31½in.) in height, we stood breathless. This happened at an antiques show in the late 1960s, where the lamp was displayed in the booth of the dealer, Glady's Koch. When we asked the price, were told that it had just been sold to the collector Paul Magriel. Later, it was one of the most important pieces in the show entitled 'Art Nouveau', organized by Mr Magriel at the Finch College Museum of Art, New York, in 1969. At that time we assured Mr Magriel that, were he ever to consider parting with the Majorelle lamp, we would love to acquire it. A few years later, he did sell his Art Nouveau collection to us, and we proudly brought his prize lamp home. When we recently sold this lamp at auction in New York, it fetched a record price for any Art Nouveau object. Although parting with the lamp was a wrenching experience at first, it pleases us to know that others now enjoy this exceptional work of art.

We are so glad that Alastair Duncan has been tenacious enough to assemble such a wealth of pictorial material and biographical information about Louis Majorelle. The many facets of Majorelle's life and works are thus illuminated for all to savour and enjoy. We can now partake of its entirety together.

New York   LLOYD MACKLOWE
February 1991   BARBARA MACKLOWE

Introduction

ANY ASPIRING BIOGRAPHER of Louis Majorelle is faced with the daunting prospect of overcoming the fact that little useful documentation, such as family correspondence, is available to flesh out the story of this outstanding Art Nouveau *maître ébéniste*. This situation is most unusual in the case of a subject who gained such celebrity in his own lifetime – a man whose career reached its pinnacle early in this century and who died as recently as January 1926. Exhaustive research draws one inexorably to the conclusion, however, that, as the result of several perverse twists of fate, no comprehensive record of Majorelle's furniture-making achievements has survived.

There are two principal reasons for this regrettable absence of first-hand biographical material. The first, and most significant, is that Majorelle's business files – his correspondence, materials and client lists, design sketches, etc. – were destroyed by the fire that consumed his workshops in Nancy in 1916. Indeed, it has to be assumed that all of the firm's files, including those of its founder, Auguste Majorelle, were centralized in the *atelier* and destroyed in the conflagration, for this provides the only credible explanation of the fact that none of the firm's records have been rediscovered by art historians during the last twenty years in the course of an often frenetic search for documentation, however minute, concerning every aspect of the Ecole de Nancy and its individual members.

The logical alternative source of biographical details – members of the Majorelle family and of the families of his employees – has proved equally unrewarding. Here, too, the researcher is confronted by an improbable series of misfortunes. Majorelle and his wife had only one child, Jacques, whose active career as an Orientalist painter was based in Marrakech, where he chose to live for health reasons and where his children were born after Louis died. Whereas Louis' brothers, Jules and Pierre, worked for the family firm during its most celebrated years, most of the other family members, including various sons-in-law, participated only after Majorelle died, and most of these died (in some instances, tragically) well before the late 1960s when a worldwide resurgence in interest in the Belle Epoque persuaded descendants of the period's pre-eminent artist-craftsmen to take steps to preserve those family records which would enhance the reputations of their forebears and, in so doing, the value of their artworks. There are, it is true, some Majorelle descendants – most, in fact, have remained in Nancy or in its environs – but not many who can claim anything more than a distant relationship to Louis Majorelle or who appear to possess significant fresh documentation concerning him or the family firm in its most fertile years.[1] Even the Musée de l'Ecole de Nancy, whose impressive collection includes many of the movement's masterpieces, and which is by definition the logical repository for documentation on Majorelle and his fellow artists, possesses no significant biographical information on Majorelle. Notwithstanding the tragic loss of original records, contemporary references (copies of many of which are on file at the Municipal Library in Nancy) do exist in sufficient numbers for it to be possible to compile a biographical account and to chronicle the introduction of the majority of Majorelle's creations.[2]

In order to gain a picture of Majorelle as an individual, and of his personality, one must rely, for the above reasons, on the written testimony of those who had close associations with him, either socially or through his business, such as Antonin Daum and Victor Prouvé, and, of course, that of his younger brother, Jules. The picture that emerges matches both the few surviving photographs of Majorelle and the portrait painted by his son – that of a gentle, sensitive, unassuming and cultivated man, whose enormous appetite and passion for work were legendary amongst his employees and competing *ébénistes*. As Jules noted in his short monograph on his late brother, published in 1927, 'As soon as the employees arrived, he was - over many years – the first at work. When clad in his great white smock, he adopts his studio attire, everything becomes enlivened by his passing by. All around the work-benches there reigns an atmosphere of trust, of respect, of admiration. Everyone knows that the advice he will give, the corrections he will make, the technique he will adjust, are all discerning. By the same token, the master placed his trust in his employees. He loves his Art, his profession.'[3]

Also in 1927, Antonin Daum paid homage, in similarly sympathetic, yet even more glowing terms, to his late friend and collaborator, 'In the name of the friends of Louis Majorelle, in the name of those who have now and then had the honour of collaborating with him, of the members of the board of management of the Majorelle firm and all friends of that establishment – only by making a huge effort can I express the sadness and the sorrow which brings us all together. But, my Friend, how could we take leave, without a word of farewell, of your smiling charm, of your artistic spirit, of your wise and weighty counsels, and without those of us who have been so close to you telling you once more what we understood and loved in you! You were endowed with all the gifts of this world, the most solemn, the most fascinating, the most delicate of feelings, the strength of character, the kindness, the authority; and none of these did you allow to be wasted. In particular you were the great hard worker . . ., the steadfast and fertile genius of an art which represents not only the glory of an epoch and the honour of the country, but the centre of an activity that is thriving and of benefit to the whole city [of Nancy]. You who were a very talented painter, learned in every aspect of art, had only understanding and encouragement for young artists.'[4]

Majorelle's success as a designer lay, in large part, in his ability, from the late 1890s, to invigorate the standard forms of eighteenth- and nineteenth-century furniture models by the introduction of subtle adjustments. His starting point was the angled, or cabriolet, front feet found on eighteenth-century furniture, such as commodes or *bergères*, which he turned further outwards. This increased curvature at the point where the piece met (and left) the ground seemed to provide it with a kind of vertical momentum. To add further to the impression of upward movement, Majorelle gave the *sabots* (toes) on the base of the feet deeply sculpted or moulded organic ornamentation. The depth of his relief detailing – usually a slightly streamlined and therefore abstracted depiction of a plant's roots and stem – was gradually reduced the higher it rose, and this helped even more to accentuate the impression of an upward flow. No longer anchored, the piece of furniture now appeared to possess a vertical dynamism, or energy, lifting it, as it were, off the ground. There remained, finally, the need to arrest this movement at a predetermined point, and this Majorelle achieved by the introduction of an upper horizontal contour – often a protruding gallery or shelf supported by an openwork strut – that provided the piece with perfect equilibrium.[5]

By this astute interplay of vertical and horizontal lines, Majorelle effected a radical change in the basic form of eighteenth-century furniture, both eliminating its static and grounded appearance, and providing it with a feeling of modernity. The introduction of luxuriant gilded foliate mounts – modelled, at their most dramatic, as life-sized water-lilies (*nénuphars*) or orchids (*orchidées*) – magnified further this sense of flow and energy, particularly when the mounts were applied vertically from the bottom up combining *sabot*, *chute* (stem) and capital. These mounts, which were unique to Majorelle amongst his contemporaries, quickly became the *imprimatur* both of his work and the entire epoch.

Majorelle's emphasis on verticality was distinctly nineteenth century in its inspiration, and quite contrary to earlier concepts, which were formulated on the horizontal line. In the course of the century, especially during the Second Empire (1852–70), the ample height of the average room afforded furniture-makers the opportunity to increase the scale of their designs. Majorelle, like his fellow makers in Nancy, Eugène Vallin and Jacques Gruber, was very prone to introducing such monumentality into his furniture, a fashion which diminished after World War I, when designers reverted to the horizontal line, and models became correspondingly lower and visually more firmly grounded.

Blessed with a superb design sense and technical virtuosity, Majorelle was simultaneously artist and artisan. Yet during his lifetime his abundant abilities were often veiled, or simply ignored, by serious magazine critics and academics because he espoused what they perceived as the frivolous Art Nouveau style. Today, however, we can judge his furniture far less harshly, and with less vitriol, than was the case in 1900, when the fundamental issue of Modernism, and of what form and direction it would take in the new century, was at stake.

In the event, the Art Nouveau movement proved, within a remarkably short space of time, to be no more than a cul-de-sac in Europe's pursuit of a twentieth-century aesthetic. Although Art Nouveau was the victim of fundamental design flaws, frequently identified and discussed at length in the press at the time, this does not, of course, prevent a positive assessment today of Majorelle's individual contribution to the history of French furniture design, as well as his other accomplishments, notably in the design of light-fixtures. Few pieces from any period can challenge the majesty of his desk *aux orchidées*, in amaranth embellished with gilt-bronze mounts and twin corolla glass lampshades, which made its début in Paris at the 1903 Salon d'Automne. Equally spectacular was his model for a grand piano, for which he retained his Ecole de Nancy colleague, Victor Prouvé, to design decorative friezes. Many other masterpieces, enriched with gilded mounts and/or marquetry panelling, punctuated the flood of *de luxe* furnishings which the family firm manufactured under Louis Majorelle's stewardship during its golden years, the decade between 1900 and 1910. To today's observer, many of these challenge the finest work by Cressent, Riesener, Du Bois and, later, Ruhlmann. Their powerful proportions and designs, lavish mix of materials and impeccable craftsmanship, place them beyond their specific style and era, and in the permanent hierarchy of the French decorative arts.

A blanket-chest with marquetry decoration
by Louis Majorelle, *c.* 1900–05.

1

Auguste Majorelle and the family firm

AUGUSTE-CONSTANTIN MAJORELLE, the father of Louis, was born in Lorraine at Lunéville. Auguste's brother was later elected mayor of Lunéville, but he himself moved in 1856 to nearby Toul, where, within two years, he had set up in business and married Marie-Jenny Barbillon, a local girl born in 1838 or 1839. As a dealer in and manufacturer of art objects, Majorelle *père* was typical of his profession in the second half of the nineteenth century, offering a selection of household decorated wares either purchased from other manufacturers or made by himself. By 1860, when he moved to Nancy and opened a tiny shop and *atelier* opposite the school of forestry in the Rue Godron in the suburb known as the Faubourg Saint-Pierre near the city boundary,[1] Auguste Majorelle had fathered his first child, Louis, born several months earlier in Toul on 26 September 1859. The other children, all born after the move to Nancy, included three sons – Jules, Achille and Pierre – and three daughters – Rose, Jeanne and Camille – and an eighth child, not mentioned in later family records, who apparently died in infancy.[2] Later in the lives of the seven children, the exhaustive personal details recorded by convention on French marriage and death certificates in the early 1900s show that Louis was described as an artist, and Jules and Pierre as industrialists, though nothing is known of Achille beyond the fact that he died before 1912. The sisters all married locally: Rose to Henri Schaeffer, Jeanne to Paul Guyot, and Camille to Raymond Dastros.[3]

As a merchant Auguste Majorelle was known principally for his faience – blank vessels purchased from nearby potteries and decorated by him – although contemporary records show that he also worked with leather, particularly in its decoration and its application to horse-drawn carriages. By the early 1860s he had extended his repertoire to include furniture – if not its actual manufacture, at least its ornamentation. Like most *ébénistes* at the time, Majorelle specialized in historic revivalism, specifically the re-creation of Louis XV and Louis XVI prototypes. Although practically all of his early creations have either disappeared or remained unidentified, a rendering dating from 1866 preserved in the Nancy Municipal Archives shows a predictable, and predictably lacklustre, copy of an eighteenth-century *rocaille* model with carved and gilded ornamentation. During this period Majorelle provided a lacquered finish to much of his furniture, in the manner fashionable amongst most contemporary cabinetmakers.

Ceramics remained Majorelle's *forte* throughout the 1860s, however, and his display at the 1868 Salon de la Société des Amis des Arts, held in Nancy, included a

Left
Auguste Majorelle, portrait in oils by
Charles Sellier, 1870s.

Right
Camille Majorelle, youngest sister of Louis,
portrait in oils by Emile Friant, 1888
(112 × 84.5 cm; 44 × 33¼ in.).

wide variety of pottery vessels with painted decoration, which were shown alongside wares produced by the Faienceries de Saint-Clément and the Cristallerie Baccarat, respectively the region's foremost manufacturers of decorative ceramics and glassware.[4]

In the 1870s, Majorelle focused increasingly on producing furniture, which remained revivalist in form and adornment. By mid-decade he abandoned lacquer in favour of varnish, an alternative finishing process, claiming that he had rediscovered the lost formula for the technique perfected in France by the four Martin brothers in the eighteenth century, and known as *vernis Martin*. Majorelle's panels *à la vernis Martin* were decorated with genre scenes in eighteenth-century style, in the manner of Watteau, Fragonard and Boucher, on a gold ground. For this work, Majorelle employed a handful of decorative painters, mostly from Paris, who were described by a contemporary commentator as *'grivois'* ('saucy') rather than vulgar.[5] Clearly, in this type of furniture manufacture, in which the wide surface areas were painted, the quality of the types of wood which Majorelle selected was only of secondary importance.

At an exhibition entitled *Rétrospective d'art lorrain*, held in 1875, Majorelle included two vitrines intended 'for displaying carved ivory'.[6] The event served as a rehearsal for the Exposition Universelle held in Paris three years later, at which Majorelle showed his ceramics and furniture alongside the work of such celebrated regional artist-craftsmen as Théodore Deck, from Guebwiller in Alsace, M. d'Huard from Longwy, and the Gallé-Reinemer firm from Nancy, all of whom, like Majorelle, presented pieces in the prevailing Oriental style. Chinoiserie enjoyed a great vogue during the Third Republic from 1870, as did Japonisme from 1867. Manufacturers at the time made precious little distinction between the two, however. A flood of wares embellished with pastiche decoration featuring Far Eastern motifs were eagerly acquired by an undiscriminating consumer market.

During his early years, the young Louis had attended school in Nancy, spending some of his free time in his father's workshop, which had been expanded and moved to the Rue Girardet. As if to confirm his elder brother's innate artistic temperament and commercial abilities, Jules Majorelle recorded that, at the age of eleven, Louis sketched a pigeon which he then modelled in clay, producing a limited ceramic edition that 'sold well'. At school, Louis studied under Messrs Larcher and Devilly,[7] and showed a great aptitude for the plastic arts.

The 1878 Exposition Universelle provided Auguste Majorelle with his only opportunity to show his wares at an international level. Amongst his ceramics and furniture, pride of place was reserved for a grand piano built by Mangeot Frères of Nancy in collaboration with the American firm of Steinway (this instrument now being in the collection of the Musée de l'Ecole de Nancy). Majorelle decorated this piano in the same typically hybrid Oriental manner. The feet were fashioned as giant Chinese Fu dogs, and the case was painted with carp, herons and other standard Japanese motifs. Although to the modern eye the composition seems to lack vitality and originality, at the time it no doubt contributed to the jury's decision to award Majorelle a Medal of Honour.

Unfortunately, Majorelle had little time to savour this success, for next year he died at the relatively young age of 54. A surviving portrait reveals a fully bearded and benign countenance closely resembling that of his son Louis when he in turn reached middle age.

Cabinet in Louis XVI style, mahogany and rosewood with lacquered panels depicting poppies; this piece, dating from the 1870s or 1880s, may be the work of Auguste or Louis Majorelle.

In the late 1870s new trends within the world of the decorative arts were still a full decade away, and Auguste Majorelle's mixture of creations must be judged within the artistic context of the time. The next opportunity for one individual to influence an entire generation of artist-craftsmen would be for his son to exploit.

In closing this chapter, it is interesting to note the remarkable parallels between the industrial art business of the Gallé and Majorelle families. These, which began with the two fathers, Charles Gallé and Auguste Majorelle, continued through the lifetime of their sons, Emile Gallé and Louis Majorelle, and well beyond. Charles Gallé and Auguste Majorelle both moved from neighbouring towns (in 1845 and 1860, respectively) to Nancy, where they established nearly identical businesses in the same district of the city. Both were commercial artist-decorators and shopkeepers who specialized first in the production of period revival ceramics and then of furniture. Both also created closely-knit family operations which their wives helped to administer; even after being widowed (in the case of Mme Gallé, also after the death of her son), both women remained active in the family business. In each case the founder was succeeded by his eldest son, who at first continued the firm's production of historically inspired wares before embracing a modernist style. And after the deaths of Emile Gallé and Louis Majorelle, respectively, other family members kept the two firms in operation for longer than they should have, at least from an artistic standpoint.

Opposite
1 *Portrait de mon père*, portrait of Louis Majorelle by his son Jacques, oil on canvas, 1908. The painting, measuring 112 × 84.5 cm (44 × 33¼ in.), was exhibited at the 1910 Salon de la Société des Artistes Français in Paris; it is now in the collection of the Musée de l'Ecole de Nancy.

J. Majorelle
Nancy 1908
portrait de mon Père

2 Grand piano built by Mangeot Frères and Steinway, with
decoration in the Oriental style by Auguste Majorelle; originally
shown at the 1878 Exposition Universelle in Paris, it is now in the
collection of the Musée de l'Ecole de Nancy.

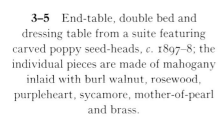

3–5 End-table, double bed and dressing table from a suite featuring carved poppy seed-heads, *c.* 1897–8; the individual pieces are made of mahogany inlaid with burl walnut, rosewood, purpleheart, sycamore, mother-of-pearl and brass.

6, 7 The Villa Majorelle (built 1901–2), present-day interior views
showing original and replacement features: (*above*) the fireplace in the
salon with later mosaic stained-glass panels by Jacques Gruber
designed after World War I; (*opposite*) the dining room, showing the
central free-standing fireplace and chimney in glazed stoneware by
Alexandre Bigot and two of the four upper transoms in stained glass
by Jacques Gruber.

8 Bedroom suite originally designed by Louis Majorelle for his villa. After his death the suite was transferred to the home of his son Jacques in Marrakech; it was acquired in 1982 by the Musée de l'Ecole de Nancy.

9 The console in the salon of the Villa Majorelle, with matching carved and marquetry decoration of pine branches and pine-cones which was the unifying theme for the room.

Opposite
10 Detail of the base of the staircase in the Villa Majorelle; designed by Henri Sauvage, the staircase features carved ivy as its decorative motif.

2

Louis Majorelle: the early years, 1880–1899

AUGUSTE MAJORELLE'S DEATH in 1879 placed his widow in a very difficult position, with a large family to raise and the business to administer. The eldest son, Louis, had been admitted on 22 March 1877 to the Ecole des Beaux-Arts in Paris, where he was studying painting and architecture under the tutelage of, amongst others, the renowned artist Jean-François Millet, whose *atelier* he frequented.[1] Louis had made his Salon début in 1875, and was progressing with merit in his chosen field; as a result of his father's death, however, he was immediately recalled to Nancy, so bringing his studies in Paris to an abrupt end.

Not yet twenty years old, and still without practical experience, Louis now took over the artistic direction of the firm. This, presumably, entailed the day-to-day supervision of the production of its repertoire of period revival furnishings, principally models in Louis XV and XVI styles. There is no evidence of any attempt by him within the next few years to make a stylistic break with precedent, and one must therefore assume that he spent the early 1880s familiarizing himself with all aspects of his adopted *métier*, especially that of the mastery of the technical skills required in cabinetmaking. In 1926 Alfred Lévy, who joined the firm in 1887 as a trainee designer and subsequently spent his entire career with it, recalled the young Majorelle's indefatigable drive and ambition: 'Endowed with an energy and a will aided by his remarkable ability to adapt and to interpret, he soon felt restricted by this studio which he considered inadequate for the future he was planning.'[2] Any initial bitterness Louis may have harboured against his family at being obliged to forfeit his membership of the vibrant community of Paris was presumably sublimated by hard work and the challenge presented by his new responsibilities. Certainly, at the time, he could not have perceived his new destiny with the same degree of enthusiasm as would have inspired him in his chosen role as a student painter.

At some point in these years, after his return to Nancy, Louis began his courtship of the young Marie Léonie Jane Kretz (born on 6 December 1864), the daughter of the Director of the municipal theatres and his wife. The couple were married on 7 April 1885.[3] Their only child, Jacques, was born on 7 March 1886.

No records appear to have survived of Majorelle's progress between 1880 and 1885, beyond his participation in an exhibition held in 1883 at the Ecole des Beaux-Arts in Nancy, in which he included what was described by a reviewer simply as an 'astonishing' piece inspired by the theme of Don Quixote.[4] Three years later, he

(*Above and opposite*) Louis Majorelle and his wife Jane, undated photographs.

presented a 4-panel screen, decorated for him in eighteenth-century style by the brothers J. & L. Voirin, local artists who had earlier carried out similar work for his father. Two other artists (who were also friends), Emile Friant and Camille Martin, also provided painted ornamentation for the firm's furniture, just as they had previously done for Auguste Majorelle. Clearly, these were not years of artistic innovation for Louis Majorelle, but rather ones in which his prime concern was keeping the firm operative and profitable. Reproductions of period models, a predictable commodity, remained its stock-in-trade. It was left to others to pursue the new trends that would soon challenge the *status quo* in the style of home furnishings.

Amongst the innovators, Gallé had by the mid-1880s emerged as the region's unchallenged leader of stylistic reform. A half-generation older than those who in the 1890s were to follow his pursuit of a new grammar of decorative ornament – that of Nature and *L'Art Nouveau* – Gallé stood practically alone during the decade, both as a theoretician of change and as a virtuoso craftsman. Whereas others in the region drew praise from year to year – such as Théodore Deck for his invention *c.* 1885 of a turquoise-blue pottery glaze, termed *bleu Deck*; the glass artist, Charles Champigneule, from Metz, for his painted windows; and René Wiener, for his tooled leather – it was Gallé whose exhibits and articulate pronouncements galvanized the local critics, who, in turn, helped to propel him, and the movement he headed, to international prominence and acclaim.[5]

Gallé's evolving quest for an art form based on Nature was endorsed at the time by the renewed stylistic vogue in Lorraine for Japonisme. An exhibition held at the

Musée des Beaux-Arts in Nancy in 1887 featured the works of the Japanese painter Takashima Hokkai, who lived in Nancy between 1885 and 1888, and this helped to focus the art world's attention on the Oriental preoccupation with outdoor themes.[6]

Three further treatises on Nature, published at roughly the same time, helped to promote Gallé's crusade. The first, by the author and critic Charles de Méixmoron de Dombasle, was entitled *Le Paysage d'après Nature*. Two others, written in Paris by P. Plauszewski in 1890, were on the same theme, *Plantes et fleurs décoratives de plein air* and *La Plante ornementale*.[7] It was under Gallé's stewardship alone, however, that the new aesthetic was ushered into the new decade, where it quickly achieved legitimacy as *the* decorative style through which art could ally itself with industry.

As noted, Majorelle appears to have been no more than an observer during these seminal years of the Art Nouveau movement. His first opportunity to participate in it was the 1889 Exposition Universelle in Paris. Ten years had passed since his father's death and the beginning of his own management of the family firm. His only recorded exhibit – an extravagant sleigh bed that evoked memories of the bizarre confections and phantasmagoria of King Ludwig II of Bavaria, rather than suggest a disciple of the new modernism – showed how entrenched still was neo-classicism's hold on him.[8] At the Exposition of 1899 Gallé was awarded the Grand Prix for his glassware and a silver medal for his painted 'low-priced furniture and *de luxe* pieces' (group III, class 17). Following this broad success of Lorraine's leading craftsmen, Roger Marx proclaimed, in his review of the Exposition, the formal renaissance of the decorative arts there.[9]

By 1890, Louis had begun the production of furniture decorated *à la vernis Martin* and to experiment tentatively with naturalism. Old and new styles were juxtaposed in the firm's display in its new showroom in the Rue Saint-Georges, which was run by his mother. In 1892 Louis was joined by his brother, Jules, and the firm was renamed Majorelle Frères. Jules' role was to assist his mother, the artistic aspect of the business being the responsibility of Louis. Perhaps in anticipation of the need to modernize his existing plant at 3 Rue Girardet in order to embrace the coming Art Nouveau style, which brought with it not only new forms but new cabinetmaking techniques, Majorelle now replaced many of his conventional hand-crafting processes with the medium's most recent forms of mechanization, describing his production methods as 'semi-industrial'.

The real Majorelle story began in 1894, with his display at the Exposition d'Art Décoratif et Industriel Lorrain, held in Nancy in June–July at the Salle Poirel.[10] Here, alongside works by Gallé, Prouvé, Martin, Friant, Daum and Champigneule, Majorelle revealed for the first time his adoption of the new aesthetic. While reaching forwards, however, he nevertheless clung steadfastly to the past by also including a whole range of period revival furniture. Among the twelve pieces listed in his display, only four appear to have incorporated modern influences: a table, a storage cabinet, an *étagère* and a *meuble à miroir*. Two of these pieces, one featuring painted floral ornamentation, were designed by Majorelle himself, and one each by Camille Gauthier and Jacques Gruber, two of Majorelle's young decorative artist colleagues in Nancy. A fifth piece, which drew the critics' praise and was later identified as *the*

Buffet with carved decoration and *chinoiserie* panel *à la vernis
Martin*, probably executed in the 1890s; and (*right*) sleigh-bed
shown in Paris at the Exposition Universelle, 1889.

work that launched Majorelle's career as an Art Nouveau exponent, was a table
entitled 'La Source' ('The Spring'). This was a hybrid creation combining
Renaissance form with a marquetry top enriched with naturalistic motifs and
including lines from a poem by Théophile Gautier,

> *Peut-être deviendrai-je un fleuve
> Baignant vallon, rochers et tours.*

The remaining seven pieces, all designed by Majorelle himself, were variously
described in the exhibition catalogue as being in Empire style, Louis XV style, Louis
XVI style, or having the characteristic features of indigenous furniture of Lorraine.
The Louis XV revival pieces included panels painted *à la vernis Martin*.[11]

The table called 'La Source' signalled to the press Majorelle's initiation into
membership of the new Modernism. The transition soon became evident both in the
new forms of the firm's furniture, and, more readily, in its choice of floral decoration,
which was now applied as marquetry rather than in paint. The far greater number of
published illustrations of pieces designed by Majorelle in the second half of the 1890s,
as compared with those showing his earlier creations, make it possible to trace his
evolving Art Nouveau style. Pieces produced immediately after 1894 were profusely
embellished both with compact floral or landscape marquetry panels and with carved
detailing on the structural supports. The effect is often overly heavy and/or clumsy
and cluttered, reminding one that these works were, in effect, 'Victorian', and, as
such, represented faithfully the period's preoccupation with lavish and extravagant
ornamentation.

(*Left*) Buffet with carved and marquetry decoration, *c.* 1899;
(*centre*) cabinet in carved pearwood with marquetry panelling,
exhibited at the Salon des Champs-Elysées, Paris, 1896; and (*right*)
armoire with carved and marquetry decoration, *c.* 1899–1901.

Absent from these creations was the prominence which Majorelle would soon
afterwards accord to bronze mounts on his furniture. Although now botanically
inspired, so as to conform stylistically, the mounts were primarily functional rather
than decorative, their visual presence being further reduced by their placement on
elaborately carved and veneered grounds.

Many of these works dating from 1895 to 1899 lack the distinction of Majorelle's
later creations. Clearly Art Nouveau in inspiration – often too much so, in fact – the
designs are attributable to several of Majorelle's cabinetmaking peers in Nancy, such
as Gauthier and Hestaux, in terms of their large scale and bloated forms. Although
tantalizingly close to his mature works, Majorelle's 1890s creations did not reveal
until practically the last moment the qualities that gave rise to his overnight triumph
at the 1900 Exposition Universelle.

In 1897–8 Majorelle inaugurated his comprehensive new workshops in the Rue
du Vieil-Aître, moving further from hand-crafted methods to industrialized
procedures. By this time he had gathered around him the first members of the team of
skilled artisans who were to share with him the successes and accolades of the new
century. Among them were Alfred Lévy (design), Charles Jung (cabinetmaker), Jean
Keppel (wrought iron), Henri Vaubourg (marquetry), Alfred Lognon (metal founder
and chaser), and Frédéric Steiner, François Louis and Eugène Gatelet (sculptors).[12]

Above and far right
Two *étagères* with carved and
marquetry decoration including inlays
of metal and mother-of-pearl, 1898.

Centre
Etagère with carved and marquetry
decoration, *c.* 1898–9 (*above*), and
cabinet 'La Cascade' with carved
decoration and marquetry panels, a
piece exhibited in collaboration with
Camille Gauthier at the Salon de la
Société des Artistes Français, 1899.

Buffet 'L'Automne', oak with carved and marquetry decoration,
shown at the Exposition Universelle, Paris, 1900.

3

The Exposition Universelle (1900) and the fruits of success

AS A RESULT of the Exposition Universelle of 1900 Majorelle was catapulted to international fame, thus establishing him as the pre-eminent *ébéniste* of his time. The critics wrote ecstatically of his furniture-making achievements, a phenomenon which was quickly labelled '*Majorellisme*'.[1] This, they found, provided – after a long and barren period of a hundred years, during which historic revivalism had prevailed within the decorative arts at the expense of new creative ideas – a direct link to France's rich eighteenth-century cabinetmaking legacy.

The new celebrity bestowed on Majorelle at the Exposition was further enhanced by its unexpectedness. Whereas his work immediately prior to 1900 had laid the foundations for a successful showing and for the public to focus their attention more narrowly on *his* furniture, as distinct from that of Gallé and the other exhibitors from Nancy, the range and quality of his display on this occasion appear to have taken everyone completely by surprise. Gallé's dominant position, in particular, had overshadowed the achievements of his disciples throughout the 1890s, reducing many of their creations to the 'school of' category or, even, to a blanket anonymity, and by the late 1890s Majorelle had only just begun to establish a reputation in the public's mind as an artist-designer in his own right.[2]

A review of the furniture which Majorelle displayed in the course of the two years immediately prior to 1900 shows, in this respect, that the technical workmanship and style of his works were sufficiently superior to those of other cabinetmakers in Nancy to ensure that the pieces he displayed at the Exposition were accorded an individual identity and enhanced status. No commentator, however, seemed to have anticipated the importance, and subsequent impact, of his display, which swept all contenders aside, both in Nancy and Paris. No doubt this was in part because Majorelle managed to maintain a veil of secrecy over those pieces which he had designed specifically for the Exposition, several of which, in the intricacy of their hand-crafting, showed evidence of enormous, and lengthy, preparation.

Majorelle's display was incorporated in the decoration and furniture category, 'Décoration et Mobilier' (group XII, class 69), which was housed in the Palais des Arts Décoratifs on the Esplanade des Invalides on the Left Bank. His works included a comprehensive array of furniture types – ensembles for the bedroom, dining room, salon, and office-library; this varied display afforded Majorelle the opportunity to introduce a broad range of sumptuous veneers, which were blended by means of the most accomplished cabinetry techniques. Pride of place in the display was reserved

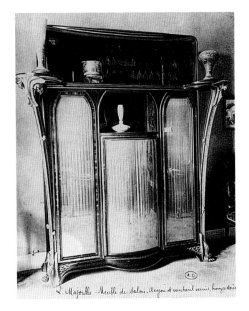

(*Left*) Salon cabinet *aux nénuphars*, mahogany and courbaril with
gilt-bronze mounts, shown at the Exposition Universelle of 1900;
(*centre*) cabinet with carved and marquetry decoration, *c.* 1900;
and (*right*) desk-bookcase with carved decoration and marquetry
panels depicting poppies and a landscape, *c.* 1901.

for the series of library and salon furniture which he had embellished with gilt-bronze
mounts modelled as life-sized water-lilies, *nénuphars* (see chapter 5). The spectacular
scale and grace of these mounts, the inspiration for which the critics were quick to
trace back to prototypes found on eighteenth-century Bourbon furniture, astonished
visitors to the Exposition.[3]

To demonstrate his versatility, Majorelle presented a bedroom suite in which the
complexity of the marquetry ornamentation rivalled the impact of the water-lily
series.[4] With decoration based on the theme of orchids (*orchidées*), the individual
pieces in the suite featured a colourful mosaic inlay of exotic woods and encrustations
of mother-of-pearl inset in fillets of brass and other metal, the fineness of which would
meet a jeweller's standard for precision. Within the suite the orchid motif was
incorporated into bold sprays of blossoms radiating across the decorative panels
applied to each piece, and was echoed both in the embroidery on the upholstery of the
chairs and in the carved detailing that outlined the contours of the furniture. The
background surfaces were likewise veneered, in thuya and exotic woods, with a
parquetry pattern that resembled horizontal bands of stylized peacock feathers or
fish-scales (the latter has since become the generic term used to describe this form of
ornamentation, which was frequently included on Majorelle's high-quality
furniture).

(*Left*) Cabinet, mahogany and red palmwood, with carved and
marquetry decoration, *c.* 1901; (*centre*) vitrine, mahogany and *bois
des îsles* with decoration including carved nasturtiums and floral
motifs in marquetry; and (*right*) oak *credenza* with decoration of
carved convolvulus and marquetry panels, shown in Paris in 1900
at the Exposition Universelle.

A measure of the general antipathy towards France's cabinetmakers at the
Exposition was provided by the critic G. M. Jacques in his review of the furniture
display on the Esplanade des Invalides. Noting with regret that, as in the 1889
Exposition, the majority of the pieces shown had represented merely slavish copies of
earlier styles, he considered the presentations of those designers who pursued new
forms to be equally flawed. Dividing the exhibition into two broad categories, he
wrote, 'The one is made up of a sort of mixed bag of borrowings from all the old styles,
blended into a copious sculptural sauce, the ingredients for which are purchased
cheaply by the maidservant at the corner grocery. The other is the "modern style", . . .
its products reveal here and there threatening tentacles ready to capture any
foolhardy person who comes near. We revolve within a vicious circle. The public at
large has no wish to break away from the old styles because nothing else that is good is
offered to them; the majority of makers refuse to attempt anything new because the
public does not want to break away from the old styles. And everybody is right.'[5]

Among the aspiring modernists, Jacques identified the works of Majorelle,
Bénouville and Bellery-Desfontaines as being the most successful. Of these, Majorelle
was without doubt the outstanding exponent, despite the obvious stylistic
transgressions introduced by his embrace of the Art Nouveau style and its utilization
of naturalistic motifs. While praising Majorelle for his fertile imagination, artistic

authority and technical mastery, he was nevertheless careful to spell out his reservations, noting that 'the principle of drawing upon natural forms, which is that of M. Majorelle, is in my eyes a great mistake. But such is the opulence with which M. Majorelle bases his works on this principle that now and then when I consider them I almost ask myself if it is not I who am mistaken. What is certain is that no artist, either French or foreign, comes anywhere near him in this field, not by a long way.'[6]

Majorelle's triumph at the Exposition led to a predictable honour from the French State, that of being appointed a Chevalier de la Légion d'Honneur, a distinction also enjoyed by others within the contingent from Nancy, especially Gallé, whose exhibit reconfirmed his dominant position in the realm of glass-making.

On their return to Nancy, those aspiring modernists who had rallied to Gallé's radical cause in the previous ten years banded together formally on 1 July 1901, to

Left
Buffet, oak with pierced decoration and marquetry panels with inlaid ebony, chestnut, maple and palisander, and gilt-bronze drawer-handles.

Opposite
Credenza with pierced decoration, marquetry panel and gilt-bronze drawer-handles.

create the Ecole de Nancy. The School's charter, published in the *Bulletin des sociétés artistiques de l'Est*, listed its aims as being: to create a professional school of instruction for the industrial arts; to found a museum, library and permanent collection; to organize lectures; to publish a bulletin; and to arrange exhibitions and competitions. Gallé was elected President, with Prouvé, Majorelle and Daum as Vice-Presidents.

A year later, Majorelle's furniture continued to generate ambivalent reactions amongst those critics who sought to reconcile the obvious excitement generated by his pieces with what they perceived as his clear violation of the established tenets of cabinetmaking. Admitting that Majorelle was, 'in a word, the outstanding figure [among makers of] modern French furniture of the costly and decorative kind', Octave Gerdeil felt it necessary, in *L'Art décoratif*, to qualify this opinion in the face of

Cabinet *aux nénuphars*, mahogany with marquetry decoration and gilt-bronze mounts.

Bookcase-display unit with carved decoration and marquetry
door-panel depicting aquatic plants.

the obvious contradictions which he perceived in his analysis of it from a traditional
standpoint: 'To discuss M. Majorelle's productions in this review is a delicate task. On
the one hand, many of them have faults which have always been criticized in terms of
principle here and which we cannot possibly approve of, even in the work of a
talented maker. On the other hand, M. Majorelle's œuvre taken as a whole reveals
qualities so rare and so numerous, stands out due to a superiority that is so obvious,
and various features of it reflect French taste so splendidly, that one must feel respect
– indeed, sympathy – for it. As far as I am concerned, I have on many occasions begun
to reproach myself for not criticizing those aspects of M. Majorelle's work which I
disapprove of; but it has the better of me – I feel I have to like it all the same.'[7]

To Gerdeil and other commentators, the Ecole de Nancy's choice of forms
borrowed from Nature as its principal means of artistic expression was permissible

(*Left*) Salon cabinet with carved and marquetry decoration; (*above*) cabinet with carved and marquetry decoration and bronze mounts, shown at the Exposition de l'Ecole de Nancy, Paris, 1903; and (*right*) *étagère* with carved and marquetry decoration.

for *other* disciplines within the decorative arts, but such decoration was not appropriate for furniture. For Gallé and Daum, in their glassware, and Lalique and Fouquet, in their jewellery, Nature proved an admirable and inexhaustible source of inspiration, but these were regarded as lesser crafts which lacked the venerable grandeur forged through the centuries between the nation's *ébénistes* and their Royal patrons. For this reason, Majorelle's furniture remained problematic, for in order to qualify as a legitimate successor to its eighteenth-century forebears it had to be judged by two time-honoured criteria: first, on its basic form, and, second, on his choice of ornamentation.

On the issue of form, Majorelle was judged largely to have circumvented the obvious pitfalls created by the Art Nouveau movement in its choice of Nature as its preferred source of formal imagery, though this could not be said of most members of the Ecole de Nancy, in whose furniture designs the basic form was often subordinated to surface ornamentation. In his own designs Majorelle kept within judicious limits in formulating the basic shape of each piece. Gallé, by contrast, was a prime culprit in this respect, for in his passion for embellishment he would often violate the fundamental architecture of his furniture. The eglantine (dog rose) cabinet which he showed at the 1900 Exposition Universelle provided Art Nouveau's detractors with

Vitrine with carved and marquetry floral decoration.

41

ample ammunition to criticize the movement's extravagances.[8] Fashioned to resemble a flowering bush, the superstructure of the cabinet was made to resemble a dense mass of entwined branches and blossoms that had little to do with the art of cabinetry. Several years earlier, Gallé's introduction of his dragonfly *guéridon*, in which the insect's thorax had been magnified to the proportions of a table leg, had drawn similar censure from the critic for *Le Figaro*, who wrote that Gallé had sacrificed logic and coherence to his love of the outdoors. Raoul Aubry's observations, made in an article published by the gallery La Maison Moderne in Paris in 1901, were typical of the contemporary reaction to such excess. He commented that the decoration 'takes precedence to the detriment of the functional aspect of the furniture', and cited the 'poppy' chair among many other examples.[9]

Majorelle, by contrast, ensured that the shapes of his pieces corresponded to their intended function. Whereas the contours and structural elements of his pieces were organic, an overall integrity of form was maintained. Thus, a chair designed by him was readily identifiable as such (it was also, and equally importantly, designed to be comfortable); a Majorelle chair did not resemble a tree or shrub in blossom – the kind of design which would cause one to sit down with trepidation in order to avoid discomfort or conceivably, even, risking bodily harm. The same was true of his

Opposite
Two *armoires* with carved decoration
and bronze mounts: (*left*) 'Passiflores',
and (*right*) *aux algues.*

A showcase at the Exposition de
l'Ecole de Nancy, Paris, 1903, in which
a selection of table-lamps produced
jointly by Majorelle and Daum Frères
are displayed.

designs for large storage units – such as armoires, bookcases, buffets and cabinets. In each instance, despite the fluid and naturalistic flow of its overall design, the outline and the placing of individual components within a given piece afforded easy recognition of its intended function.

On the second issue, however, that of his choice of decoration for pieces of furniture, Majorelle was judged to have strayed from convention. His landscape and floral marquetry panels were considered trite and immature ('*enfantin*') in their literal attempts to recreate painted landscapes. They were, in short, too bland and undistinguished for the art of marquetry. Such reproduction of works painted on canvas using wood as a medium was not art. In this context Octave Gerdeil stated without equivocation that 'the very compositions which provide the basis for these marquetries are, from the decorative point of view, defective. Instead of being synthetic and providing rhythmic outlines, they are diffuse, muddled, lacking punch. Indeed, I regret to have to say that they are the least pleasant aspect of the art of Nancy.'[10] Gerdeil did, however, acknowledge Majorelle's sensitivity to the problem of how best to apply non-traditional ornament to a traditional medium, and his subsequent search for acceptable solutions. 'He has kept the use of natural imagery within sensible limits in the decoration of his furniture, and in terms of the way in

43

Two vitrines with carved and marquetry decoration; the example above is of burl maple.

which he adapts it, a pleasing inventiveness of a personal kind is guided by a feeling for the established principles of furniture. For example, he takes roots or the base of the trunk as his point of departure in the search for a shape for the feet of a piece of furniture, he is careful not to try to recall the natural organic form as his compatriots would do, and in its place substitutes – with elegance and never-failing ingenuity – a purely technical form.'[11]

Such criticism remains valid today, particularly when one considers the striking effect produced by Majorelle's use of gilt-bronze mounts as compared with the labour-intensive and time-consuming process of veneering. The mounts were quicker and easier to manufacture, less expensive (when produced in multiple editions), and their visual impact was more spectacular than that of marquetry panels.

Majorelle himself realized this after 1900, perhaps in part by taking into account some of the critics' comments and in the maturing of his own artistic taste. From then on, gilt-bronze mounts were introduced increasingly (at the expense of marquetry) as the primary means of ornamentation. The surfaces of panels in furniture were now

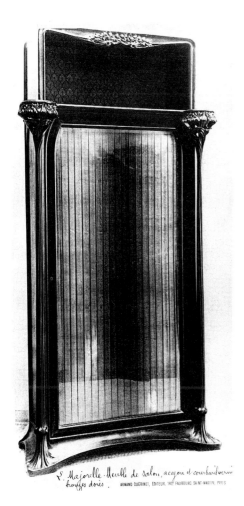 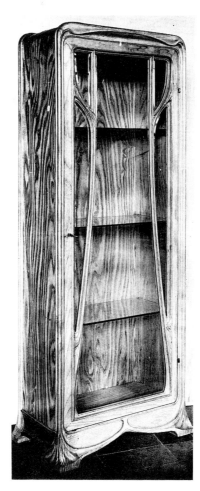 

(*Left*) Salon cabinet, mahogany and courbaril with carved and marquetry decoration; (*centre* and *right*) a vitrine and a cabinet, both with carved decoration.

(*Left*) Cabinet bookcase *aux orchidées*, amaranth with gilt-bronze mounts, exhibited at the Salon de la Société des Artistes Décorateurs, 1910.

(*Above*) Vitrine *aux orchidées*, mahogany with gilt-bronze mounts.

left bare; the quality of the wood employed and the richness of its grain provided beauty enough. Gerdeil's assessment had been correct: the aesthetic impact of Majorelle's furniture was enhanced when it excluded veneered decoration.

The critics found it impossible not to draw comparisons between Majorelle and Gallé. Whereas Majorelle lacked Gallé's passion for nature and intellectualism, he was clearly the more accomplished cabinetmaker. He also, as noted above, adhered to the traditional rules of furniture design passed down through the centuries, whereas Gallé was a persistent transgressor. Gallé went about the task backwards, transforming trees into pieces of furniture *before* considering their intended function. Beyond this fundamental difference, Gallé's designs were invariably lighter, both

Cabinet *aux orchidées* with carved decoration and gilt-bronze mounts.

literally and visually, than those of Majorelle. They tended, also, to be smaller in scale and lighter in colour (Gallé utilized a range of pale fruitwood veneers, which contributed to this difference). Gallé's furniture designs, finally, were often more delicate and, indeed, more precious and 'feminine' than those of Majorelle.

Even before 1900, Majorelle had begun to establish a distribution network beyond Nancy. A magazine advertisement in 1898, designed by Henri Bergé, listed the firm's outlets in Contrexeville (Vosges), Cannes (Alpes-Maritimes), and at 56 Rue de Paradis, Paris. A showroom was opened in 1901 in Lyons at 28 Rue de la République. Two others, inaugurated presumably at about the same time or slightly later, were listed on the firm's stationery in 1910: in Lille (55 Rue Esquermoise), and Paris (22 Rue de Provence). Another, in Cannes (46 Rue d'Antibes), appeared in the firm's literature after World War I. A further Majorelle outlet (later and undated) was given as 53 Avenue Victor Emmanuel III, Paris.

The Paris address was clearly a prestigious one, linking Majorelle more directly to the international market. The initial showroom in the Rue de Paradis was replaced in 1904 by the firm's purchase of Samuel Bing's celebrated gallery, La Maison de l'Art Nouveau, at 22 Rue de Provence, in the 9th *arrondissement*. Bing, who had been the most articulate and ardent promulgator of the new movement, became bankrupt in 1903. On 29 June 1904, plans by the architects Pierre Selmersheim and Henri Sauvage for the conversion of Bing's gallery (originally designed by Louis Bonnier in 1895) into Majorelle's Paris headquarters were revealed. At the time little was said in the press either about the success of this venture, or later about the expanded premises taken over – at no. 126 in the same street – by Majorelle between 1911 and 1913.

In addition to maintaining these furniture outlets, Majorelle remained an active member of the annual Paris Salons from the mid-1890s until his death in 1926. He was a member of four – those of the Société des Artistes Décorateurs, the Société des Artistes Français and the Société Nationale des Beaux-Arts, as well as the Salon d'Automne – and believed, presumably, that the display of his latest creations at the Salons, alongside those of his cabinetmaking rivals, brought his work to the attention of an audience wider than those who only visited his showrooms.

Throughout his career Majorelle drew on a wide range of wood veneers; his initial selection was extended from the late 1890s following France's colonization of various North African countries, as a result of which the number of exotic species available to the nation's cabinetmakers was increased. Mahogany, courbaril[12] and amaranth remained his favourite choices until World War I, their interchangeability for important pieces or suites of furniture being often seemingly arbitrary. Other species used intermittently included walnut, palisander, purpleheart, thuya, bougainvillea and teak, several of the latter group being used specifically to introduce the range of textures and colours required for his marquetry work. As a general rule, warm, reddish hues were chosen for bedrooms, to create a feeling of comfort and intimacy, and dark-brown or black hardwoods for more masculine preserves such as offices, smoking rooms or libraries. His preferred decorative motifs, invariably botanical, matched the repertoire utilized by most of his colleagues in the Ecole de Nancy.

48

Bookcase *aux algues* with carved decoration and wrought-iron mounts.

Two cabinets *aux algues*, both with carved decoration and
wrought-iron mounts; the example above was exhibited at the
Salon de la Société des Artistes Décorateurs, Paris, 1906.

These included clematis, fern, water-lilies, seaweed, orchids, convolvulus, hawthorn, pine-cones, satin-pods (honesty), bell-flowers (campanula), silphium and arrowheads.[13]

Through these years several individual works and/or furniture series emerged as *tours de force*, not only within Majorelle's total œuvre, but of the entire Art Nouveau era. The passage of time has afforded today's historian a clear view of these: in particular, his series of grand pianos for Erard, introduced at the 1904 Salons;[14] his dining-room suite *aux tomates* introduced in the same year; and, of course, the numerous pieces in the water-lily and orchid series (from 1900 and, roughly, 1903, respectively). To these must be added a selection of Majorelle's light-fixtures (see chapter 6) as representative of his most spectacular creations.

These masterpieces were manufactured in small editions – *'les petites séries'*, as Majorelle termed them – each limited to four or five examples. This was the procedure followed by most industrial artists at the time, including Gallé in his glassware and the Daum glassworks in theirs. In many cases, after the original work had been designed and executed for a specific client, a further handful of examples were made (these would differ from the original only slightly, either in matters of artistic interpretation or in hand-crafted detailing). Whether Majorelle was obligated in such cases, or merely felt it was his duty, to consult the original client about his decision to reproduce the commissioned piece in a later edition is unrecorded. The sale of limited editions brings to mind the issue of Majorelle's role as an industrial artist, and of how he reconciled himself to playing a dual role as an individual designer and a commercial artist.

The years 1900–08 were a golden era for Majorelle, during which piece after piece of breathtaking quality came on to the market.[15] The 1900 Exposition Universelle was followed by two further important events, the first in Paris in March 1903, held in the Pavillon de Marsan at the Musée de l'Union Centrale des Arts Décoratifs in the Rue de Rivoli (now the Musée des Arts Décoratifs), in which Majorelle's entry formed part of an exhibition staged by the Ecole de Nancy.[16] Majorelle displayed some twenty-two items, which included a suite of salon furniture with water-lily decoration; a wrought-iron vitrine filled with examples of his metal key-plates; seat furniture and a pedestal table (*guéridon*); and a selection of table-lamps.

The following year, the Ecole de Nancy was host to another exhibition of modern decorative arts, on this occasion in the Galeries Victor Poirel in Nancy.[17] For this, Majorelle prepared an extensive range of his creations, including a complete room setting which took account of every detail, including the manufacture of a ceiling corner light-fixture in stucco, wall fabrics, a stained-glass window by Jacques Gruber, and a chimney surround with painted panels by Charles de Méixmoron de Dombasle. Another ensemble, intended for a study, featured pieces in mahogany and courbaril and included a desk with orchid motifs, bookcase, chairs and a chimneypiece featuring *bas-relief* decoration by Ernest Bussière. A selection of table-lamps – with botanical themes including umbel-shaped shades, as well as thistle, arrowhead. water-lily and magnolia – demonstrated his preoccupation with the lighting of his room settings.

Louis Majorelle, undated photograph.

Also in 1904, Majorelle exhibited in the United States, at the St Louis World's Fair (French section, groups 14 and 38) and on this occasion he was awarded a grand prix for his office and home furnishings. In the same categories, Gallé and Alfred Lévy received silver medals.[18]

During the next three years Majorelle appears to have participated only at the Paris Salons. In 1908 his work was shown in an exhibition in Strasbourg (then in Germany), staged by the city's Société des Amis des Arts at the Palais de Rohan between 7 March and 26 April.[19] The firm showed a diverse range of furnishings: a bedroom and study with seaweed motifs: a selection of orchid and fern furniture; and diverse works in wrought iron.

In 1909 the Exposition Internationale de l'Est de la France, staged in Nancy, brought the curtain down on the Art Nouveau movement locally, and with it, the Ecole de Nancy. Even though Majorelle exhibited two of his most spectacular water-lily pieces – a desk and a double bed – both had in fact been introduced in Paris several years earlier, and therefore lacked freshness. *La Revue lorraine illustrée* provided the sole coverage of the Ecole de Nancy's exhibit, which was housed in a building designed for the event by Eugène Vallin.[20] In his review, its critic, writing almost in the past tense, was mercifully brief and nostalgic. The School had been suffering from gradual eclipse ever since Gallé's death in late 1904, a decline which accelerated after 1909 as the search for a new, and more conservative, decorative style was pursued at the Paris Salons. For his part, Majorelle eliminated from 1910 the pursuit of new Art Nouveau designs for – like his Salon colleagues – he was not really certain where the future lay. For this reason the era encompassing the years 1908 until the advent of World War I has been described by today's art historians as 'transitional'. It appears that, if Majorelle excelled at all during this time, it was in the continuing development of his work in wrought iron (see chapter 5): in 1913, the firm released information on its recently completed wrought-iron stairway and balcony for the Galeries Lafayette department store in Paris, and its stairway for the French Embassy in Vienna.[21] No mention was made of new furniture designs. Examination of the pieces which the firm presented at the Salons in these years shows, most noticeably, that the boldness and luxuriance of its gilt-bronze water-lilies and orchids had gone; their place had been taken by a wide range of lightly carved, and rather dreary and rectilinear, furniture aimed rather at a middle-class market. Like his cabinetmaking colleagues, Majorelle was forced to yield to Europe's post-1910 austerity, a period of tightening budgets that placed increasing import-ance on machine-made, as distinct from hand-crafted *de luxe*, production.

In 1912 Majorelle suffered two immense personal tragedies. The death of his mother on 24 August, at the age of 74, signalled the first of the series of reversals that would severely test his resolve over the next five years, and leave him alone (and acutely lonely) in the twilight of his life and career (although he maintained a very close relationship with his son, Jacques, the latter settled, for health reasons, in Marrakech in 1923, having spent an increasing amount of time there after his first visit in 1917).[22] Though retired for several years, Majorelle's mother had previously played an indispensable role as an administrator in the family business, both through the transitional period following her husband's death in 1879, and well beyond.

The premature death of Majorelle's wife Jane, on 31 December 1912, was an even more devastating blow.[23] Contemporary accounts attest to the exceptional closeness and happiness of the marriage, during which Mme Majorelle provided constant counsel and encouragement.

In his eulogy of his elder brother, Jules Majorelle made reference to his sister-in-law's cherished role as wife and business partner: 'All these qualities were echoed in the wife with whom Louis Majorelle shared his life. She cannot be considered separately, for her role was too conspicuous. A wonderful union bringing together two kindred spirits, as noble in character and in fine feelings as they were complete. Beautiful and endowed with a delightful character, refined equally in heart and mind, Mme Majorelle was the companion whom Louis Majorelle had to emulate.'[24]

Plates 12–93

WORKS BY LOUIS MAJORELLE

12 Buffet with carved and marquetry decoration and gilt-bronze mounts, *c.* 1900–05.

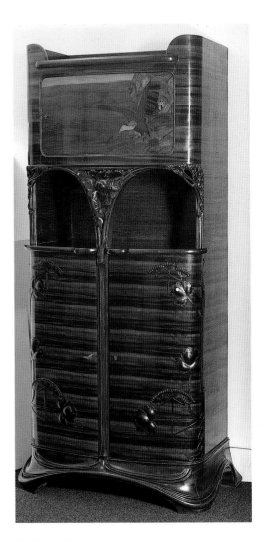

13–15 Three models presented at the 1900 Exposition Universelle in Paris: (*left*) *étagère* 'Les Baigneuses', mahogany and oak, with carved and marquetry decoration; (*centre*) *étagère* with carved and marquetry decoration and wrought-iron mounts; (*right*) cabinet 'Le Nid de l'aigle', walnut and macassar ebony with marquetry panel and wrought-iron mounts.

16 Cabinet *aux nénuphars* with tambour doors, mahogany and courbaril with gilt-bronze mounts.

17 Corner bookcase *aux orchidées*, 1905, mahogany and amourette
with marquetry panels and gilt-bronze mounts.

18 Vitrine *aux nénuphars*, mahogany with marquetry panels and
gilt-bronze mounts.

19   Cabinet *aux nénuphars*, *c.* 1904, with marquetry panels and gilt-bronze mounts.

20, 21   Large buffet (*below*) and buffet (*right*), both with 'Epis de blé' motif in carved decoration with gilt-bronze and gilt wrought-iron mounts.

22 (*left*) Vitrine *aux orchidées* with gilt-bronze mounts.

23 (*centre*) *Etagère* with carved and marquetry floral decoration.

24 Cabinet with carved and marquetry decoration and gilt-bronze mounts.

25 *Etagère* with carved decoration and marquetry panels.

Opposite
27 Buffet with carved and marquetry decoration and
wrought-iron mounts.

26 Buffet with carved and marquetry decoration and
wrought-iron mounts.

28 Corner cabinet-settee with carved decoration and gilt-bronze mounts.

29 Buffet with carved decoration and bronze mounts.

30–33 Orchid-decorated furniture

30, 31 Chest of drawers and cabinet with conforming gilt-bronze mounts.

33 Cabinet with marquetry decoration and gilt-bronze mounts.

32 *Armoire* with gilt-bronze mounts.

34 Cabinet with carved and marquetry decoration and gilt-bronze mounts.

35, 36 Buffet with carved and marquetry decoration and gilt-bronze mounts shown enlarged in the detail opposite.

Right
38 Console with large mirror and with
gilt-bronze mounts.

37 Vitrine *aux orchidées* with gilt-
bronze mounts.

39 Vitrine *aux nénuphars* with
marquetry decoration and gilt-bronze
mounts.

40–43 A cabinet with two *étagères* (*above*) and a buffet, all with carved and marquetry decoration.

Opposite
44 Cabinet 'La Mer', with carved and marquetry decoration and
wrought-iron mounts.

45 Buffet with carved and marquetry decoration and bronze
drawer-handle.

46 Desk *aux nénuphars*, mahogany with gilt-bronze mounts; this model was introduced at the Exposition Universelle of 1900.

47 Dressing table *aux orchidées*, mahogany with gilt-bronze mounts and glass lampshades (replacements).

48 Desk *aux orchidées*, mahogany and amourette with gilt-bronze mounts, *c*. 1903–5.

49 Desk *aux orchidées*, mahogany with gilt-bronze mounts.

50 Desk *aux orchidées*, amaranth with gilt-bronze mounts and opalescent glass lampshades, 1906.

51 Desk *aux nénuphars*, mahogany with gilt-bronze mounts.

52 Desk *aux nénuphars* with marquetry decoration and gilt-bronze mounts.

53 Table with marquetry decoration.

54 Table with marquetry decoration
and gilt-bronze floral mounts.

55 Two-tier round table *aux nénuphars*
with gilt-bronze mounts.

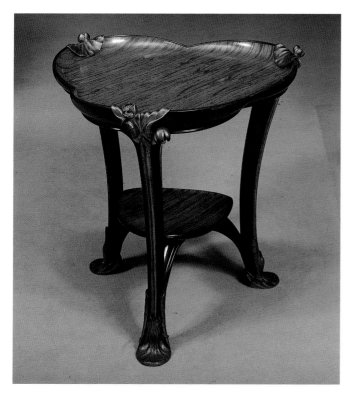

56, 57 Two-tier tripod table *aux nénuphars*, mahogany and tamarind with gilt-bronze mounts, shown at the Exposition de l'Ecole de Nancy, Paris, 1903; and (*right*) two-tier table with gilt-bronze floral mounts.

58 Two-tier table with marquetry decoration (aquatic plants) and gilt-bronze mounts (flowering rushes).

59 Settee *aux orchidées* with gilt-bronze mounts.

61 Side chair with gilt-bronze floral mounts.

60 Settee with original upholstery as shown at the Exposition Universelle of 1900.

62 Armchair and side chair *en suite*, walnut with carved decoration; both shown at the Exposition Universelle of 1900.

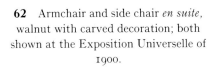

63 Desk chair *aux nénuphars* with gilt-bronze mounts and leather upholstery.

64 Side chair (detail), showing carved openwork and marquetry decoration.

65 Open-sided armchair *aux nénuphars* with gilt-bronze mounts.

66 Corner seat, walnut with carved decoration, *c.* 1900.

67, 68   Chest of drawers and bed from the bedroom suite shown at
the Exposition Universelle of 1900 (for another bed made to the same
design, see pl. 75); walnut with inlaid decoration including thuya,
amaranth, *bois des îles*, burl amboyna, mother-of-pearl, brass
and pewter.

69, 70 Two pairs of end-tables made to the same design. The examples above were shown at the Exposition Universelle of 1900 as part of the bedroom suite (see also pls. 67, 68, 71); those below are of darker French walnut with inlaid mother-of-pearl and pewter.

71 Dressing table from the bedroom suite shown at the Exposition
Universelle of 1900 (see also pls. 67–69).

74 *Armoire*, walnut with marquetry decoration; this model was shown at the Exposition Universelle of 1900.

72, 73 *Armoire* and double bed with marquetry decoration.

75 Bed, walnut with marquetry decoration; for another model made to the same design see pl. 68.

76 Double bed and end-table *aux orchidées* with marquetry decoration and gilt-bronze mounts.

Overleaf
77 Bedroom suite *aux nénuphars*, mahogany and rosewood with gilt-bronze mounts.

78 Wall-mirror, the surround featuring carved and marquetry decoration.

Opposite
80 Fireplace surround *aux orchidées* with carved decoration and gilt-bronze mounts.

79 Fireplace surround, green marble with gilt-bronze mounts.

81   Buffet *aux tomates* with carved decoration (tomatoes), silvered
bronze drawer handles and wrought-iron mounts, 1904.

83, 85 Grand piano by Erard, with carved and marquetry decoration ('La Mort du Cygne'), 1903–4.

84 Grand piano by Erard, with carved and marquetry decoration designed by Victor Prouvé, 1903; the subject is based on Richepin's 'La Chanson de l'Homme au Sable', with scenes showing a mother and child, the dying child, and the child transported by the dream, together with the verse:

Chantez, la nuit sera brève
Il était une fois un vieil homme tout noir
Il avait un manteau fait de rêve
Un chapeau fait de brume du soir
Chantez, la nuit sera brève.

86 Detail of grand piano showing carved decoration.

87 Mantel clock with carved
decoration of foliage and seed-heads.

88, 89 Pedestal case clocks with carved
decoration.

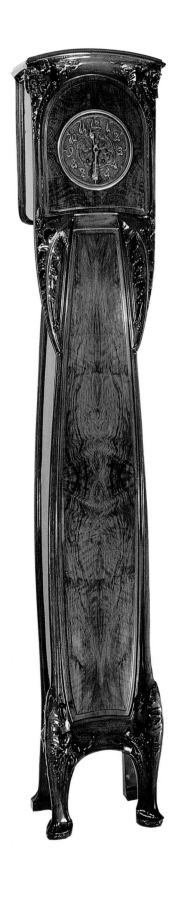

90   Mantel clock with gilt-bronze mounts (thistles).

91, 92   Pedestal clocks, one with carved decoration, the other with carved and marquetry decoration, both on botanical themes.

Detail of a headboard with marquetry
decoration of poppies.

Opposite
93 Marquetry panel showing an intricate combination of various
wood veneers and mother-of-pearl, *c.* 1901.

97

Desk, mahogany with marquetry
decoration and gilt-bronze mounts,
1901.

Desk *aux orchidées*, mahogany with gilt-bronze
mounts and glass lampshades.

Desk and wall-mounted *étagère* with
carved and marquetry decoration,
1901.

Coiffeuse aux algues with carved decoration
and twin lamps.

Coiffeuse with carved and marquetry decoration.

Desk *aux algues* with carved decoration.

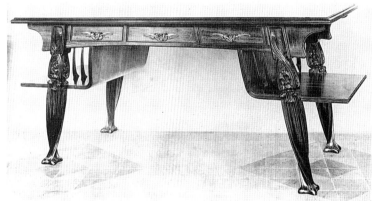

Desk *aux pins* with carved decoration.

Desk with carved and marquetry decoration.

Pedestal desk 'Junko' with carved decoration.

Dressing table/sink, mahogany and
macassar ebony with marble top and
gilt-bronze mounts.

Cashier's desk (*above and right*), walnut
with carved decoration.

Cartonnier, mahogany with carved decoration, gilt-bronze mounts and glass lampshades.

Desk and chair with carved and marquetry decoration.

Table with carved floral decoration.

Occasional tripod table with carved
and pierced decoration.

Two-tier tea table, mahogany and burl
maple with gilt-bronze mounts.

Occasional tripod table with gilt-
bronze mounts.

Pedestals with carved decoration.

Table with carved and pierced
decoration.

103

Two-tier table with gilt-bronze
mounts.

Console table, carved walnut with
marble top.

Two-tier occasional table, *c.* 1902.

Table with carved decoration and
marble top.

Left
Two tables, in mahogany and walnut
respectively, *c.* 1902.

Two-tier table with marquetry
decoration and gilt-bronze mounts.

Table with carved and pierced
decoration and quarter-veneered top.

Table with carved and pierced
decoration and marquetry top.

Side table *aux fougères*, with carved decoration and two drawers (*below*), and triple-panel cheval glass *aux clématites* with carved and pierced decoration (*right*): both pieces were exhibited at the Salon du Mobilier, Paris, 1902.

Four-panel screen, walnut with carved relief decoration and marquetry panels; this piece was shown at the Exposition de l'Ecole de Nancy, Paris, 1903.

Four-panel screen (frame only), walnut with carved decoration, *c.* 1900–05.

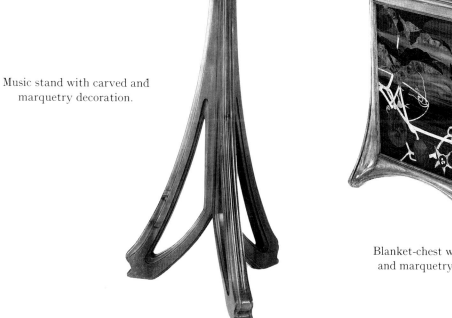

Music stand with carved and marquetry decoration.

Blanket-chest with carved decoration and marquetry top and side panels.

Settee *aux clématites* with carved decoration, shown at the Exposition de l'Ecole de Nancy, Paris, 1903.

Armchair and side chair for a salon, 1902.

Settee and armchair *aux fougères*, both of gilt wood with carved wood decoration.

Set of chairs with carved floral decoration.

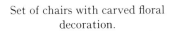

Open-sided armchair with carved and
marquetry decoration.

A selection of chairs and a settee in modern style as illustrated in
the catalogue of the Exposition de l'Ecole de Nancy, Paris, 1903.

Desk chair *aux algues* with carved
decoration.

Desk chair and armchair with carved floral decoration.

Desk chair, side chair and armchair, all in amaranth with gilt-bronze mounts, exhibited at the Salon de la Société des Artistes Décorateurs, Paris, 1910.

(*Above right*) Armchair *aux sagittaires*, with carved and pierced decoration, shown at the Exposition de l'Ecole de Nancy, Paris, 1903.

(*Right*) Open-sided armchair with carved and pierced decoration and side chair with carved decoration, both shown at the Exposition Universelle, Paris, 1900.

Settee, gilt wood with carved decoration.

Open-backed side chair, mahogany
with gilt-bronze mounts.

Settee *aux fougères*, gilt wood with
carved and pierced decoration.

Armchair with carved decoration,
1904.

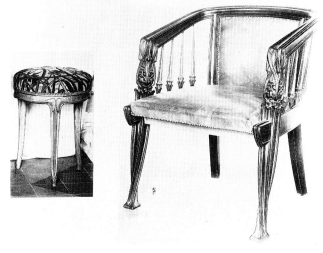

Settee *aux sagittaires*, stool and desk
chair *aux pins*, the latter shown at the
Salon de la Société des Artistes
Décorateurs, Paris, 1904.

Side chair 'Feuille de marronnier'
(chestnut leaf), walnut with marquetry
decoration.

Open-sided armchair and side chair *aux clématites*, with
conforming carved and pierced decoration.

Settee *aux pins* with carved and pierced decoration.

Bed and end-table with carved and
marquetry decoration.

Bed and end-table *aux algues* with
carved decoration.

Bed and end-table, mahogany with
carved and marquetry decoration,
1901.

Right
Armoire aux clématites with carved and
pierced decoration.

Part of the bedroom suite included in the Majorelle display at the
Exposition Universelle, Paris, 1900.

Fireplace surround 'Junko' with gilt-
bronze mounts.

Fireplace surround *aux orchidées* with
gilt-bronze mounts and with
overmantel mirror.

Cheval glass with built-in lighting at
floor level.

Fireplace surround with overmantel
mirror and *trumeau*.

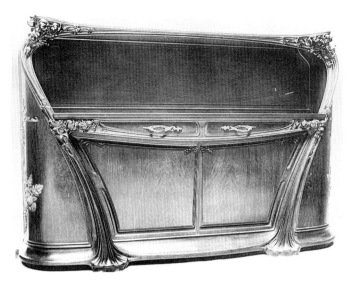

Pieces from a dining-room suite *aux tomates*, all with carved decoration: (*above*) buffet, also having silvered-bronze and wrought-iron mounts; (*below*) chairs; (*right*) dining table.

Dining table with central *surtout* having carved decoration of convolvulus flowers and foliage; the piece was shown at the Exposition Universelle, Paris, 1900.

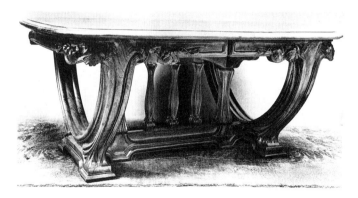

Dining table with carved decoration, exhibited at the Salon du Mobilier, Paris, 1905.

Buffet 'Vicorne' with carved decoration.

Buffet with carved and marquetry decoration.

Buffet 'La Vigne' with carved
decoration and glass panel with
wrought-iron mount.

Buffet with carved and marquetry decoration
and dining chair *en suite*, 1902.

Buffet with carved and marquetry
decoration.

114

Pedestal clocks:
(*left*) with carved decoration *aux raisins*; (*centre left*) with carved decoration *aux tomates*; (*centre right*) *aux orchidées* with gilt-bronze mounts; (*right and bottom*) with carved and marquetry floral decoration.

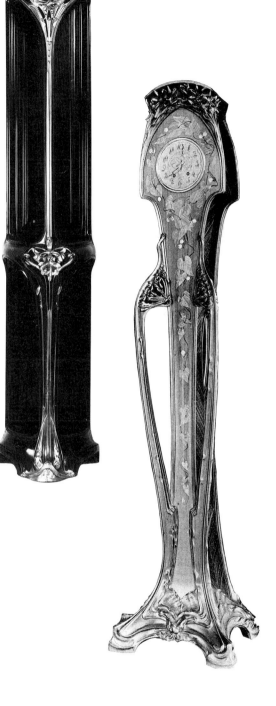

The Villa Majorelle: interior views seen in contemporary photographs

(*Top and bottom*) The salon: the fireplace is flanked by the original
stained-glass window by Jacques Gruber (destroyed in an air-raid in
1916); the entire furnishings and décor have the pine-cone as a unifying
theme.
(*Middle row*) The dining room with furniture by Majorelle having a
decorative motif of ears of wheat; the lower part of the staircase,
designed by Henri Sauvage and featuring carved decoration of ivy; and
the portmanteau/umbrella stand in the vestibule, showing the wrought-
iron coat-hooks in the form of satin-pods, designed by Sauvage and
executed by Majorelle.

4

The Villa Majorelle

SANDWICHED today between neat lines of residential buildings, the Villa Majorelle was conceived for a rural situation, to be built in grounds to the west of Nancy, in the direction of the neighbouring town of Laxou. Majorelle acquired the land in 1897 from his mother-in-law, Madame Kretz (his father had earlier purchased land in the same vicinity and in 1873 he sold it back to the city). In 1902, a critic for *L'Illustration* described the area, known as Medreville, as being 'on the western borders of the old city, in a suburb dotted with villas, the view from which takes in a pleasing horizon of wooded hills'.[1] Though it was soon encroached on, and later absorbed by Nancy's burgeoning industrial sector, the Majorelle property still maintained around 1900 a distinctly rural identity within a patchwork of irregular parcels of land, some of which were under cultivation.

Majorelle purchased the land to provide a site for a new workshop to replace the cramped facilities and outmoded equipment of his *ateliers* in the Rue Girardet. He now planned to establish a comprehensive plant, complete with the most modern machinery capable of handling the firm's diverse production in wood, metal, leather, marble, plaster, fabrics and lace. A local architect, Lucien Weissenburger (1860–1929), was retained to design the enormous new building – providing 3,500 square metres of floor space – and to supervise its construction; it was completed and operational by the end of 1898. Practically no documentation has survived concerning the *ateliers*, whose address was given as 6 Rue du Vieil-Aître. Weissenburger, a founding member of the Ecole de Nancy in 1901, and soon to be heralded as one of the province's foremost exponents of Art Nouveau with his designs for private homes, commercial buildings, department stores, hotels and *brasseries* in Nancy, was not in this instance invited to provide an architectural interpretation of the new movement's aesthetics: his brief was to design a no-frills, functional structure to house a modern industrial art manufactory.[2]

Once the new workshops were operational, Majorelle proceeded with his next project on the site: the construction of a house for himself and his family. Surprisingly, however, he turned not to Weissenburger or to another local modernist architect for the design; in the late 1890s only two other architects, Georges Biet (1869–1955) and Henri Gutton (1873–1942), had created buildings that showed a clear affinity for the Art Nouveau idiom, and the Nancy movement's most gifted exponent, Emile André (1871–1933), established himself in business only in 1901. In 1898 Majorelle's choice was a young, still unknown designer and would-be architect working in Paris, Henri Sauvage (1873–1932), born in Rouen. The Villa Majorelle was, in fact, Sauvage's first completed architectural commission. Earlier in the same year, however, he had invited Majorelle to collaborate with him on a scheme for the interior of the fashionable Café de Paris, at 41 Rue de l'Opéra, in the French capital; for this commission Majorelle provided the furniture for the 3-room restaurant, the interior of which Sauvage designed and decorated. Although this was Majorelle's first Parisian commission, he had previously submitted numerous displays to the regular annual Salons; none the less he was no doubt grateful to Sauvage for the introduction, and for the added exposure provided by the reviews of the installation which appeared in leading French magazines devoted to the decorative arts.[3] He must also have been impressed, while working on the Café de Paris project, by the young designer's obvious skills and versatility – Sauvage had trained in wallpaper and fabric design at the firm of Jolly et Sauvage (in which his father was a partner), in addition to participating in the annual Salons with displays of book illustrations, theatre and textile designs, etc.[4] Perhaps more important to Majorelle was the fact that Sauvage had studied architecture under Pascal at the Ecole des Beaux-Arts. Further, the two men had several mutual connections within the art world – for example, Majorelle had known Sauvage's elder brother while studying at the Ecole des Beaux-Arts, and his old friend Alexandre Charpentier was Sauvage's father-in-law – all of which must have contributed to Majorelle's belief that Sauvage, fourteen years his junior and unqualified as an architect, was nevertheless up to the job. Many years later at the time of the 1925 Exposition Internationale des Arts Décoratifs et Industriels Modernes, Sauvage provided his own account of the commission which effectively launched his career as a *bone fide* architect, 'He entrusted me – in 1898 – with the construction of a splendid villa in Nancy. This was, I believe, the first modern house to be built there. I worked on it for two years, revising my work a hundred times over . . . May I take this opportunity of expressing my warmest thanks to my first client for the unexpected freedom he allowed me, and for not imposing on me, despite my youth, either financial constraints or his own personal ideas.'[5]

* * *

Known also as the 'Villa Jika' (derived from the French pronunciation of the initials of Majorelle's wife, Jane Kretz), the house was built between 1901 and 1902 under the supervision of Lucien Weissenburger, who at Majorelle's request oversaw the day-to-day construction.

A comprehensive study of Sauvage's design for the villa would exceed the scope of a book on Louis Majorelle, although he no doubt collaborated closely on overall architectural considerations – specifically, the interplay of line, material and space – if only to ensure a sense of unity with the interior, which he, together with a handful of other artists working under his direction, were to decorate and furnish. On its completion, the villa was roundly applauded within the architectural community for its bold innovations at a time when neo-classicism was enjoying a significant revival in France.[6] Sauvage was perceived, in his successful marriage of architectural rationalism with a brisk, if somewhat picturesque and neo-Gothic, modernity, to be a worthy disciple of Viollet-le-Duc, who in the mid-nineteenth century had led the

The Villa Majorelle seen from the north, showing the main entrance and the terrace, and (*right*) from the south-west, with the windows of the salon in the right foreground (see plan overleaf).

fight against architectural convention, principally the idea that a building's exterior should be symmetrical. The fact that the villa's four façades were all different was not seen as incongruous or undisciplined, but rather an honest attempt to achieve an orderly and mathematical solution to its interior flow and the distribution of rooms, which were divided into three distinct areas, or 'zones for living': a service/servant area, a stairwell, and the family living quarters. The critic Frantz Jourdain, writing in both *L'Art décoratif* and *Art et décoration*, provided a perceptive analysis of the building – with its curious blend of the old and the new – following its completion in 1902. He described it as 'a dwelling that is neither lavish, nor official nor vain, a dwelling that is neither that of an upstart or of a great lord, but which still does not descend to mediocrity and middle-class banality. We recognize clearly the house of an artist of feeling and curiosity, with refined tastes, a cultivated mind and a sensitive eye, who is little concerned with the opinions of others and with fashionable snobbery, and who seeks to invest with beauty the everyday objects in which he does not expect to lose his interest.'[7] The result, he concluded, was successful because it was built 'by an artist for an artist'.

To enter the villa, the visitor passes through an outer door surmounted by a curved glass canopy attached by slender wrought-iron sprays of satin-pod (or honesty; *monnaie-du-pape*). The door itself, with matching sprays, opens to reveal a portmanteau likewise embellished with satin-pods, their stems serving as coat-hooks. A flanking doorway with silk door-hangings (now gone), which separated the kitchen area on the left from the rest of the house, repeated the theme, thereby effectively completing the stylistic unification of the transition from exterior to interior. The ubiquitous satin-pod theme was further enforced in stained-glass windows by Gruber and in miscellaneous fixtures, such as door-handles. Additional harmony was established in each of the villa's 'public' spaces by the selection of a single ornamental theme: the pine-cone (*pomme-de-pin*) for the salon, ears of wheat (*épis de blé*) for the dining room, and ivy (*lierre*) for the stairway. The repetition, in this manner, of a botanical decorative theme served both Majorelle's artistic and commercial philosophies: the creation of serial furniture to form complete ensembles.

The villa's interior is dominated by its wood-covered surfaces, particularly the panelled walls, which provided a warm and opulent ambience that was well in tune with contemporary middle-class expectations and, no doubt, those of Majorelle himself. The harmonious flow from room to room of the decoration and furnishings established the house effectively as a showroom to supplement the one in the Rue Saint-Georges – a practical demonstration for any customer of the end-result to be expected of an investment in Majorelle's fashionable brand of modernism.

In addition to Gruber, who created further unified themes for the windows in the dining room (colocynths) and salon (owls perched on fruit trees), Majorelle called on the talents of the Parisian ceramicist, Alexandre Bigot, who provided a monumental free-standing fireplace and chimney for the dining room, as well as miscellaneous decorative tiling to accent the building's stone exterior; and of Victor Prouvé, who contributed a painted frieze (now gone) in the dining room.[8] Predictably, Majorelle himself provided the villa's furniture. Contemporary illustrations of the individual rooms reveal a selection of his standard furnishings, of commercial rather than *de luxe* quality, suggesting that Majorelle used his home as a showplace to court middle-income clients rather than the wealthy élite. Perhaps he had learned from his display at the 1900 Exposition Universelle in Paris that the truly rich – those who could afford his spectacular creations featuring gilt-bronze water-lily and orchid mounts, lived in the capital rather than in the provinces.

The Villa Majorelle has survived as a prime example of high-style Art Nouveau architecture in Nancy. As such, it would have served as a highly appropriate alternative space to house the Musée de l'Ecole de Nancy, which is in fact located in Eugène Corbin's former residence in the nearby Rue du Sergent-Blandan. Today the house serves as the office of a local government body for the *département* of Meurthe-et-Moselle.[9]

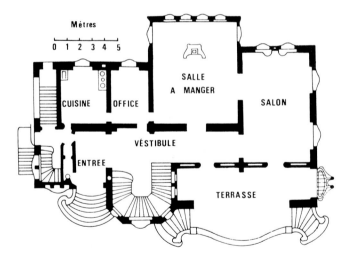

Plan of the ground floor.

5

Metalware:
bronze and wrought iron

Bronze

It is probable that Majorelle's father did not have to produce his own furniture mounts. Foundries in Paris, if not in the French provinces, catered to that section of the cabinetmaking trade which specialized in the manufacture of period revival furniture. Matching sets of *bronze doré* mounts – escutcheons, drawer-handles, hinges, capitals, *chutes* and *sabots*, mostly exact copies of seventeenth- and eighteenth-century prototypes – were available on demand from wholesalers to the trade. This supply eliminated the need for makers of furniture in Louis XV and Louis XVI styles to provide their own casting facilities, and it may be for this reason that Louis Majorelle was able to wait until 1890 before deciding to install a forge in his small cabinetry workshop in the Rue Girardet, Nancy. The date corresponds also to the time that he began to experiment with the new Art Nouveau style, a development which would require the use of floral mounts, unavailable through wholesalers, that were unified stylistically with the new movement's grammar of ornament.

Between 1890 and 1897, Majorelle's furniture – that which embraced the new aesthetic – was notable for the minimal emphasis placed on metal mounts. Decoration was provided principally by means of intricate marquetry panelling and sculpted detailing. Metal components were understated and visually undistinguished; they were merely functional appendages of secondary artistic consequence. Then, however, probably after he had opened his expanded *ateliers* in the Rue du Vieil-Aître and effectively disengaged himself from the manufacture of furniture in earlier styles, Majorelle appears suddenly to have reconsidered, and reversed, the minor role which his metal furniture mounts had played, elevating them from a humble status to one of pre-eminence. Within a year, he conceived a spectacular series of furniture based on the theme of the water-lily (*nénuphar*). Eliminated from this series, for the most part, were all marquetry and sculpted forms of ornamentation; in their place he applied gilded bronze mounts cast as life-sized water-lily plants, combining flowers, buds and stems, sweeping boldly up and along the contours of the furniture.

Conceived and perfected during 1898 and 1899, the water-lily series made its début to an astonished audience at the 1900 Exposition Universelle, when a variety of pieces were shown, in particular a desk and bookcase for a man's study.[1] The undeniable majesty and originality of the series served to crown Majorelle as the era's undisputed master cabinetmaker. Even those critics who found the mounts too bright and overbearing for their own tastes felt the need to acknowledge their dramatic impact and to concede that they provided a brilliant modern interpretation and evocation of past glories. Octave Gerdeil, for example, wrote in 1901 in *L'Art décoratif*, 'The applications of bronze, which M. Majorelle has been incorporating into this category of furniture for two or three years, are extremely well judged. My own feeling is that one should refrain from introducing metal into furniture except for locks in the strict sense; but I readily accept the skilfulness and the good taste of M. Majorelle's adaptations in metal. His choice of position, outline, patinas – all contribute to the creation of an ornamentation that is both distinguished and pleasing.'[2]

Well-versed in France's furniture heritage, thanks to his work within his father's firm, Majorelle was no doubt inspired by the ornamental emphasis placed on ormolu furniture mounts by *ébénistes* of the late seventeenth and eighteenth centuries. Today, even a cursory glance through the catalogues of the French furniture collections in, for instance, the Louvre, the Palace of Versailles, or the Wallace Collection in London, shows the infinite variety of opulent Louis XV pieces with which a cabinetmaker specializing in the reproduction of period masterpieces would have been conversant. The Majorelle studio's library would have included countless illustrations of similar period models, many of them no doubt commissioned directly by the Sun King and his Bourbon court. It is not surprising, therefore, that the inspiration for Majorelle's water-lily series is clearly discernible in the more lavish rococo creations of royal *ébénistes* such as Charles Cressent, Antoine Criaerdt, Antoine Gaudreaux, Jacques Dubois, Jacques Caffieri, and, slightly later, Jean-François Oeben and Van RiesenBurgh; all of these had created furniture which was heavily dependent, in achieving its majestic impact, on the use of extravagant gilded mounts. Impressed, if only in concept, by the decorative value and ample scale of these mounts, Majorelle set out to modify and to modernize them.

In place of the eighteenth century's somewhat scrambled iconography of gilded acanthus, palmettes, garlanded and ribboned floral swags, and miscellaneous *rocaille* decorative accents, Majorelle opted for a single motif – the water-lily – by which to accentuate the proportions of his furniture and the rich grain of its veneers. The foot (*sabot*) of each water-lily mount was transformed into the plant's bulbs and trailing roots, from which arose a tall and slender stem (*chute*) that terminated in flowers and buds to form a capital, which on certain furniture models was made to protrude diagonally on openwork supports in a bold organic sweep that captured fully the essence of the Art Nouveau style's rhythm and dynamism, a quality which completely eluded many of Majorelle's furniture-making rivals. Ancillary mounts for the water-lily series were all *en suite*: drawer-handles fashioned as curled lily-pads, and escutcheons in the form of sinuous budding tendrils enclosing the keyholes. Subtle variations occur in the designs of the water-lily mounts in their adaptation to the shape of each individual piece of furniture in the series. This, due in part also to refinements made by Majorelle after 1900, helped to provide variety by the elimination of unnecessary repetition.[3]

More recent decorative trends, beginning during the Second Empire (1852–70), i.e. the highly gilded and gaudy period revival confections typical of the traditional

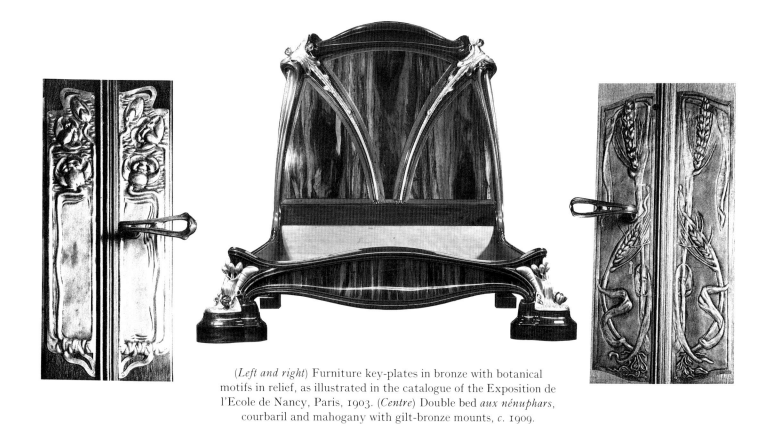
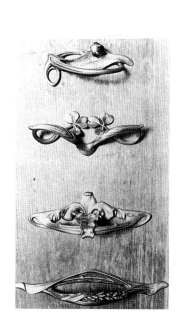

(*Left and right*) Furniture key-plates in bronze with botanical motifs in relief, as illustrated in the catalogue of the Exposition de l'Ecole de Nancy, Paris, 1903. (*Centre*) Double bed *aux nénuphars*, courbaril and mahogany with gilt-bronze mounts, *c.* 1909.

(*Left and right*) Decorative drawer-handles in bronze and gilt-bronze, shown at the Exposition de l'Ecole de Nancy, Paris, 1903. (*Centre*) *Bureau plat* with integral twin gilt-bronze lamps.

cabinetmaking district of Paris, around the Faubourg Saint-Antoine, must also have made an impression on Majorelle, if only to remind him that France's rich furniture-making legacy must provide the inspiration for every new wave of modernism. Despite the ostentation and ill-considered eclecticism which characterized most Napoleon III furniture – particularly, a flagrant disregard for artistic harmony which had led inevitably to the random interchange of characteristic motifs from different epochs – commercial cabinetmakers such as François Linke, Henri Dasson, Paul Sormani, and Alfred-Emmanuel-Louis Beurdeley still paid homage to the eighteenth century in their re-creations of its masterpieces. In these the gilt-bronze mounts were given a prominence which presumably influenced Majorelle.

The water-lily furniture, offered as individual pieces or, preferably, *en série* for libraries, salons and bedrooms etc., established itself after the 1900 Exposition Universelle as the firm's pre-eminent line, aimed at an élite international clientèle. It was followed, around 1903, by a second series based on the theme of the orchid (*orchidée*). Comprising the same capital-*chute-sabot* components, with matching foliate drawer-handles and escutcheons, the decoration was, if anything, even more lavish than its predecessor, both in its scale and in its complex pierced compositions. Other ormolu-mounted floral editions – such as hawthorn (*aubépine*), fern (*fougère*), *junko* and *attacia* – were offered by the firm, though often only for small pieces of furniture, such as tea-tables and *guéridons*, and none as spectacular.

At the same time as the water-lily edition was conceived, Majorelle provided a similarly enhanced role for mounts on most of his furniture, including a range of medium-priced designs. The mounts were always carefully scaled, however, so as to avoid creating an imbalance with the other forms of ornamentation, such as marquetry panels and carving, that featured in these pieces.

Curiously, or perhaps significantly in view of the highly distinctive design of Majorelle's furniture, none of his cabinetmaking colleagues in Nancy or Paris attempted to emulate his water-lily and orchid mounts. Although Vallin and Gruber frequently created monumental pieces which, in their scale and bold sweeping contours, resembled a similar range marketed by Majorelle, they preferred deeply carved ornamentation to the use of applied metal mounts. For his part, Gallé had a predilection for floral or landscape panels and *bas-relief* carved detailing. His bronze mounts, used especially for key-plates and drawer-pulls, were more precious and less ambitiously proportioned than those of Majorelle, and were invariably finished not in gold but in a brown patina that blended better with the wood's lighter surface colour and texture. In Paris, the Art Nouveau style was interpreted by Hector Guimard, Eugène Gaillard, Georges de Feure and others with greater fluidity and subtlety; its depictions of nature were confined to slender intertwined plant motifs of a more abstract kind that were carved, rather than applied by way of marquetry panels or metal mounts. The water-lily and orchid series therefore survived as an unmistakable signature of Majorelle at his most brilliant, a proud and highly distinctive *imprimatur* both of its maker and of the Belle Epoque.

By 1910, when the public's disenchantment with Art Nouveau's excesses had led to the movement's demise, Majorelle realized that the earlier popularity of his *de luxe* editions had likewise waned. Following his displays of a study featuring orchid decoration at the Exposition Internationale de l'Est de la France in 1909, and the following year at the Salon of the Société des Artistes Décorateurs in Paris, neither it nor the water-lily series was reviewed in contemporary art magazines.[4] In the same manner that the ormolu excesses of Louis XV's *ébénistes* had precipitated their own fall and the search for a less exuberant style under Louis XVI, so Majorelle's gilded age gave way to a more restrained and less expensive period governed progressively by middle-class tastes and purses.

Only one of Majorelle's bronze workers is mentioned by name in contemporary exhibition catalogues; Alfred Lognon was listed in 1904 as a bronze chaser, and in 1919 as a caster.

Wrought iron

Towards 1900, the iron industry transformed the Lorraine landscape, as the traditional wood-fired forges were supplanted by large smelting works that met much of Europe's iron requirements. The existence of rich mineral deposits throughout the region created industrial development in or near Nancy, Longwy, Briey, Pompey, Maxeville and elsewhere, attracting national, Franco-Belgian and Franco-German concessions to extract the ore. This, in turn, spawned a secondary industry of iron- and steel-works, refineries and foundries that sprang up in the vicinity of the mineshafts. The local press heralded a new Iron Age, one that helped to advance wrought iron's legitimacy beyond its hitherto conventional use in engineering and architecture, in which it had always been employed principally for structural elements.

For those in Lorraine in search of an inspired decorative precedent for iron beyond these preserves, there was one outstanding ironsmith, Jean Lamour (1698– 1771), whose œuvre was inextricably bound to the region's artistic heritage, and who therefore served as the inspiration for artist-craftsmen of the late nineteenth century. Lamour's accomplishments as a *ferronnier* dwarfed those of all of his successors. Especially celebrated was his ornamental grillework in the Place Stanislas in the heart of Nancy, and many of Lamour's creations were already preserved in local museums, such as the Musée Lorrain, where they were on view to those who spearheaded the revival that the medium enjoyed at the *fin de siècle*. The previous decades had witnessed a procession of undistinguished works in iron, principally architectural components such as grilles and railings, that displayed neither taste nor originality. On a national level, the renaissance was credited to the Parisian Emile Robert, who in the 1880s elevated the medium to the point where it would soon rival bronze as the metal most favoured in the field of the industrial arts – a field in which the latter's sovereignty had previously been unchallenged. This would take a while longer, however, and Robert's early ornamental ironwork remained mostly within the confines of traditional uses – as exterior grilles, window-guards, balconies, railings and canopies.

The advent of modernism, with its grammar of floral ornament, led Robert to seek the artistic collaboration of Victor Prouvé on several commissions.[5] Prouvé, as mentor to the younger generation of artist-craftsmen who later formed the nucleus of the Ecole de Nancy, no doubt disseminated information on Robert's progress to his fellow artists in Nancy, alerting Majorelle, amongst others, to the resurgence and expanded potential of wrought iron.

The earliest reference to Majorelle's work in this medium appears to have been in an article published in *La Lorraine artiste* in 1899, which referred to banisters and lamps recently completed by him.[6] The specific mention of lamps indicates that he began to incorporate wrought iron into his furnishings at roughly the same time (though probably slightly later) as he began to explore the wider use of bronze.

In the opinion of several critics, Majorelle's ornamental wrought iron found its finest expression in his light-fixtures, the majority of which featured blown-glass shades incorporated into the existing wrought-iron armatures by Daum glassworks. The latter were designed by Majorelle mostly as attenuated flowers and plants, which, with their fluid plasticity, belied the rigidity of the material. This, in turn, helped to provide wrought iron with a 'personality' distinctly different from that of bronze. Deftly planished tendrils and foliage were so natural in appearance as to conceal the nature of forged metal. Rapid technical advances at the time – changes that would soon render obsolete the medium's traditional tools, the hammer and anvil – enabled Majorelle's ironsmiths to achieve an artistic finish comparable in quality with the crisply chased detailing found on his bronzes.

Majorelle's architectural wrought-iron creations were limited largely to commissions in Nancy and neighbouring towns. Notable examples in Nancy were: his own house, the Villa Majorelle (1901/02; see chapter 4); the Hôtel Bergeret, 24 Rue Lionnois (1904); the Chambre de Commerce, 40 Rue Henri-Poincaré (1908); and the Banque Renauld, 9 Rue Chancy (1910).[7] Beyond Lorraine, the staircase and balcony which he executed a few years later for the Galeries Lafayette department store in Paris proved to be his most monumental achievement in metal. Several of these architectural works were embellished with decorative accents in polished copper. These were often composed of chased and *repoussé* flowerheads or foliage that sprouted from entwined and undulating stems. The result is invariably rich and graceful in its effect. Preferred indigenous plant motifs – fully consistent with the standard botanical repertoire embraced by the Ecole de Nancy – included: satin-pods (honesty), umbels, cereals, roses, thuya, maple, *samares* and ferns. A series of wrought-iron furniture mounts were designed also in the form of aquatic plants, including seaweed, arrowheads (*sagittaires*) and *calla palustris* (of the Arum family), the last two endemic to lakes in the Vosges region.[8] Majorelle's interpretation of these plants was invariably more abstract, and robust, than that employed by Gallé on his furniture.

Wrought iron won an increased role in Majorelle's production after 1900, and was boosted once again after World War I with the firm's introduction in 1920, at the Salon d'Automne and at that of the Société des Artistes Décorateurs, of a series of *verreries ferronnées* – vases, bowls and lamps – consisting of glass by Daum blown into

The interior of the Galeries Lafayette, Paris, *c.* 1913, showing the wrought-iron staircase and balcony railings by Majorelle.

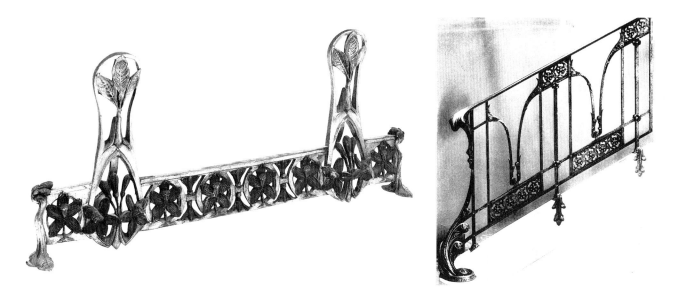

Andiron, parcel-gilt wrought iron.

Staircase balustrade in wrought iron as exhibited at the Salon de
la Societe des Artistes Décorateurs, 1900.

hammered wrought-iron armatures.[9] Conceived by Majorelle during the war years, the linear designs of these wares corresponded to the Art Deco high style that would dominate the Paris Salons for the next five years. Curiously, these mounts often appear crude today when compared with the finish on the firm's earlier metalware, perhaps a consequence of a shortage of raw materials and technology in the aftermath of the war. Often visually heavy and revealing a coarsely hammered finish (now frequently corroded), these pieces bear a distinctly commercial look uncharacteristic of the firm's standard output.

Examination of Majorelle's furniture, to determine his preference on occasion for wrought-iron mounts over bronze, reveals no clear pattern beyond the fact that the former seems to have been used mostly in conjunction with deep-brown or black woods, including rosewood, walnut and, in the 1920s, macassar ebony. The metallic lustre of iron, the surface of which was sometimes treated with a patina or lacquer to lend it an artificial appearance of age, complemented better the granular surfaces of dark veneers than those of lighter ones, for which bronze mounts, either patinated brown or gilded, were preferred. Also, the hammered surface texture of iron possessed a distinctly rigorous, or 'masculine', look, that blended well with the over-sized furniture, such as bookcases and storage units, which Majorelle designed for largely male preserves such as libraries, smoking rooms and offices. A typical example of this type of furniture was the firm's 'Pavillon de Marsan' bookcase, a monumental unit with correspondingly large and robust iron hinges. Other editions, such as Les Algues' (seaweed) and 'La Vigne' (the vine), featured similar hand-wrought applied mounts.[10]

Little is known about the individual artists in the Majorelle metalshop. Listed through the years as *ferronniers* in the firm's entries in exhibition catalogues were Jean Keppel (1904), Desgrey (1919) and Mahier (1925).

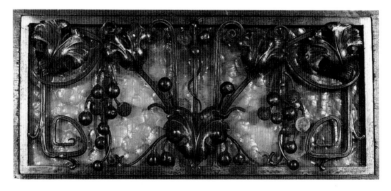

Detail of a vitrine *aux raisins*, wrought-iron over pale-purple textured glass.

Opposite
94 Detail of bookcase showing gilt-bronze corner mount imitating orchid flowers and foliage.

128

95, 97 Water-lily corner mounts in gilt-bronze seen on a vitrine and on a writing desk, both *c.* 1900–2.

96 Base of standard lamp with fern-shaped gilt-bronze supports.

98 Hinges and mounts on a buffet *aux tomates*, wrought iron, *c.* 1904.

99 Cabinet 'La Mer' with wrought-iron mounts, 1905.

100 Entrance to the Chambre de Commerce et d'Industrie, Nancy, 1908, showing wrought-iron gates and glazed *marquise*.

Opposite
102 Detail of staircase balustrade in the Banque Renauld, Nancy, 1910; wrought-iron with satin-pod motifs and gilt-bronze rail and detailings.

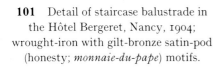

101 Detail of staircase balustrade in the Hôtel Bergeret, Nancy, 1904; wrought-iron with gilt-bronze satin-pod (honesty; *monnaie-du-pape*) motifs.

103, 104 Selections of vases combining wrought-iron armatures by Majorelle and glass by Daum, *c.* 1920–2.

105 Table-lamp with floral decoration *aux ombelles*, wrought-iron base and etched Daum glass shade, *c.* 1903.

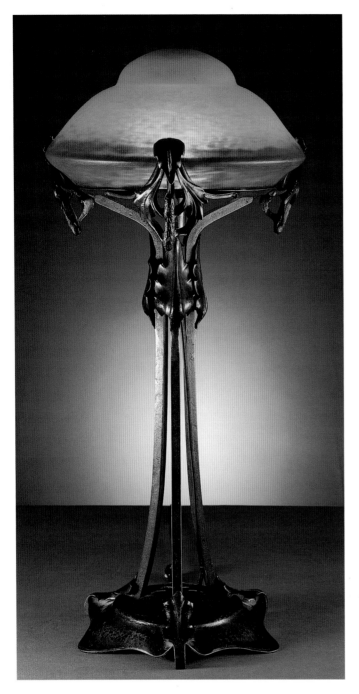

106, 107 Table-lamps combining wrought-iron bases and Daum blown-glass shades.

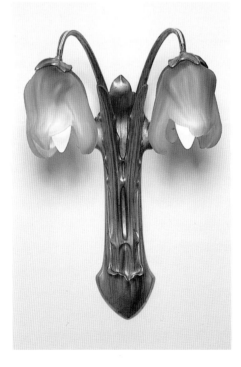

108 Wall-sconce with twin lamps, gilt-bronze and flower-shaped blown-glass shades.

109   Table-lamp, parcel-gilt bronze
base and blown-glass shade.

110   Table-lamp, gilt-bronze base and
glass shade etched with bat motif.

111   Table-lamp with wrought-iron base in the form of dandelion
leaves and stems and with triple blown-glass shades with etched
decoration in imitation of dandelion seed-heads.

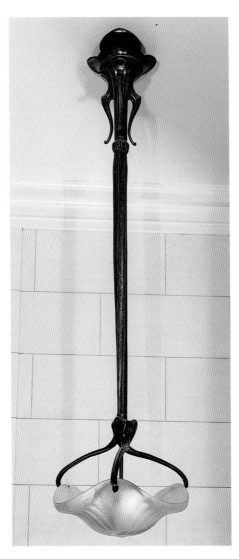

112   Ceiling fixture, bronze with blown-
glass shade.

113   Ceiling pendant, gilt bronze with
blown-glass shade.

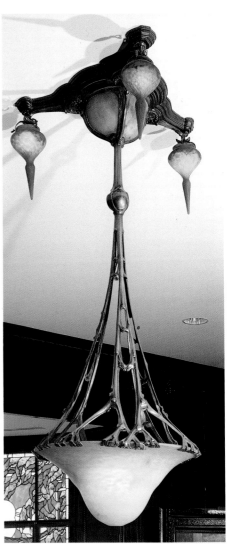

115   Ceiling fixture, gilt bronze with
blown-glass shades.

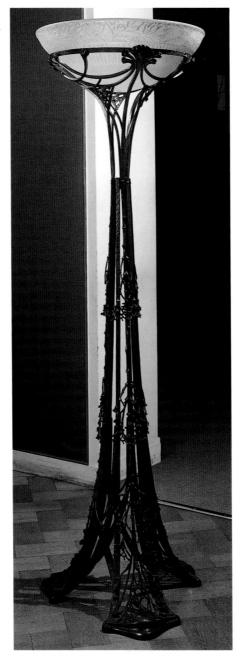

114   Standard lamp 'Poincaré', c. 1914,
wrought iron with blown-glass shade, in
the Musée de l'Ecole de Nancy.

116 Pair of wall-sconces, bronze with glass shades.

117 Table-lamp, wrought-iron base with blown-glass shade.

118 Table-lamp, wrought-iron base with blown-glass shade in the form of an open flower-head.

119 Standard lamp, wrought-iron base with blown-glass shade.

120 Table-lamp, bronze base with blown-glass shade, *c.* 1903.

121 Ceiling fixture, wrought iron with opalescent glass shades and circular stained-glass panel, *c.* 1906.

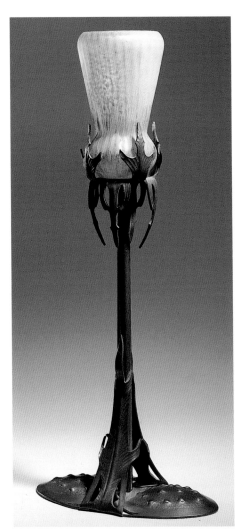

123 Table-lamp 'Chardon' (thistle), wrought-iron base and blown-glass shade, *c.* 1904.

122 Table-lamp, bronze and opaque blown-glass shade with *appliqué* beetle motifs.

125 Table-lamp, wrought-iron base and blown-glass shade.

126 Table-lamp, wrought-iron base and blown-glass shade, *c.* 1903.

124 Table-lamp, wrought-iron base and blown-glass shade.

127 Table-lamp 'Cactus' with base and stems of bronze and floral shades in blown glass, *c.* 1903.

128 Table-lamp, gilded wrought-iron base and twin blown-glass shades, *c*. 1903.

129 Table-lamp 'Perce-neige' (snowdrop), wrought-iron base and blown-glass shade, *c*. 1905.

132 Table-lamp 'Nénuphars' (water-lilies), bronze base with triple multi-coloured glass shades, *c*. 1903.

130 Table-lamp, bronze base and blown-glass shade, *c*. 1900.

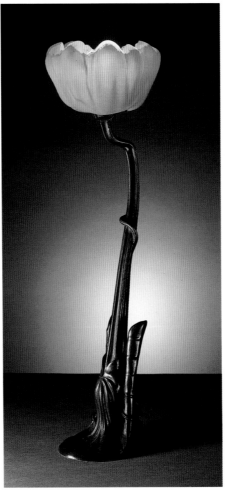

131 Table-lamp, bronze base and glass shade (an open water-lily), *c*. 1903.

133 Table-lamp, wrought-iron base with blown-glass shade, *c.* 1903.

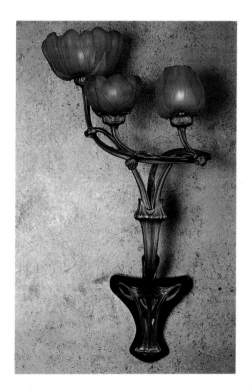

134 Wall-sconce, gilt bronze with triple glass shades in the form of magnolia flowers.

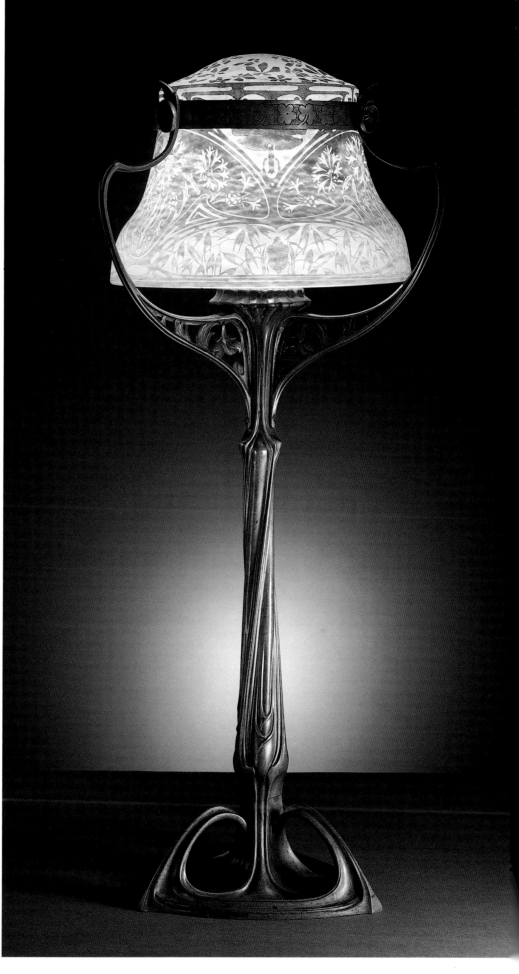

135 Table-lamp, bronze base with patterned glass shade, *c.* 1903.

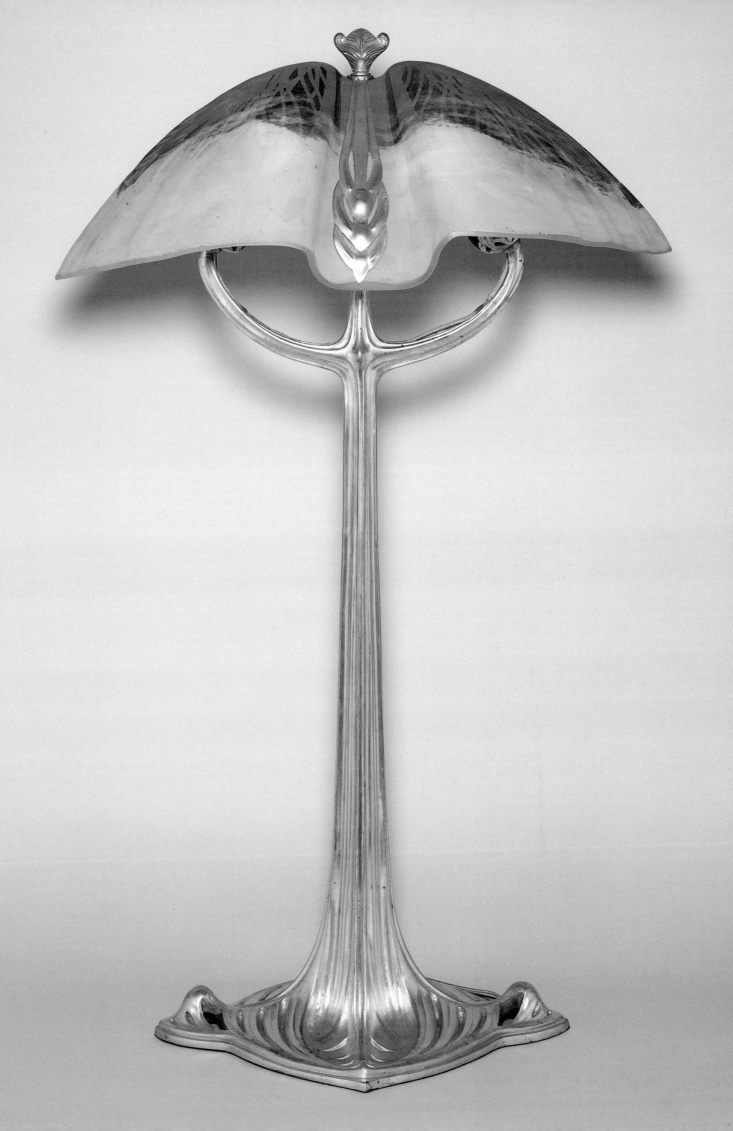

6

Lighting

THE COLLABORATION between Majorelle and the Daum glassworks, which apparently began shortly after the latter's inception in 1891, proved to be a source of mutual satisfaction and commercial benefit to both firms. Clearly, however, it was Majorelle who stood to gain the most from this arrangement, for there were other metalworkers within Nancy and neighbouring Lorraine who could just as easily have produced lamp mounts of acceptable quality in either bronze or wrought iron for Daum (the metalworker J. Cayette, amongst other individuals and foundries, provided bronze mounts for Nancy lamp designers at the turn of the century, including, on occasion, Gallé).[1] Conversely, no other glasshouse could have matched either the artistic creativity or the skilled artisanship achieved at the Daum glassworks (the sole exception was, of course, Gallé, who tended not to collaborate in this manner with his fellow decorative artists in Nancy).

Together, the two firms produced a prodigious number of light-fixtures in a joint venture that spanned three decades. There are no surviving records to show who designed the individual models, which were promoted by both firms. Were the designs for the spectacular Art Nouveau water-lily and magnolia table-lamps, for example, conceived by Louis Majorelle alone, or in collaboration with Auguste or Antonin Daum? Certainly, there must have been close technical collaboration between the firms in their creation, but was there also artistic teamwork? Most of the important lamps included in this book were credited to Majorelle not just by contemporary critics, but in entries in the catalogues of the Ecole de Nancy's own exhibitions and of the various Salons at which they were displayed. Other models, made entirely of glass (except for minimal metal mounts), were likewise illustrated by the Majorelle firm in its catalogues without any acknowledgment to the Daum glassworks, which clearly executed them. Examination of the Daum archives does little to resolve the issue, for these records include other models that were credited elsewhere to Majorelle, in addition to featuring most of the all-glass designs which appeared in the Majorelle firm's promotional literature.

Majorelle found his inspiration for his lamp designs in numerous indigenous plants, including aquatic species. Those most suitable for the purpose consisted of slender stems or branches, with a single flowerhead or a small cluster of blossoms. The hollow lamp-base, within which the electric wire was concealed, was sculpted naturalistically to form the plant's stem which supported the glass shade(s) in the shape of flowerheads. In each case the result – whether with a bronze or a wrought-iron base – invariably possessed an exquisite elegance, thus ensuring that the piece

(*Above left*) Chandelier, early 1900s; the wrought-iron fixture features sprays of satin-pods and is embellished with glass lampshades and a circular leaded stained-glass panel.

(*Above right and opposite*) A selection of table-lamps with glass shades by Daum, some with etched decoration, others in the form of flowers. All date from *c.* 1903–05 except the slightly later thistle lamp opposite, made *c.* 1905–10, which features a wrought-iron base with gilded crosses of Lorraine (the thistle is the emblem of Lorraine).

would blend harmoniously into period settings. Majorelle also designed a variety of lamps having undecorated domed glass shades that were interchangeable with his flower-form shades. Although these designs have unimpeachable refinement and dignity, they lack the dynamism of models based on natural forms.

Majorelle exhibited his lamp models both as individual pieces – alongside his furniture at the Salons – and as constituents of ensembles unified by a single botanical theme. The majority of his finest models were created between 1902 and 1910, and displayed both at the annual Salon d'Automne and at those of the Société des Artistes Français and the Société des Artistes Décorateurs.[2] Writing about one such display in 1908, the critic for *La Revue lorraine* noted with enthusiasm, 'The standard lamps created by him are delightful in their originality; here there is a Nepenthes leaf whose pitcher, made of opal glass, is intended to hold the light; in another case there are three dandelion seed-heads of varying heights rising above jagged-edged Taraxacum (dandelion) leaves; let us end by mentioning yet another candelabrum with energetic lines bearing three elegantly proportioned Magnolia flowers.'[3]

Today, one must question how successful many of these lamps were in fulfilling their intended purpose, whether to provide direct light for reading or to illuminate a painting or some other treasured object. As with most Art Nouveau lamp creations, which used Edison's newly commercialized filament light-bulbs having a consumption of only 7 or 10 watts, Majorelle's models did little more, in reality, than illuminate themselves. Like the electric lamps of Louis Comfort Tiffany or Emile Gallé, they became self-illuminating *objets d'art*, having no great practical value because their shades of opalescent glass trapped most of the light produced. Only the light which was emitted directly up and/or down was of any practical use. Today the

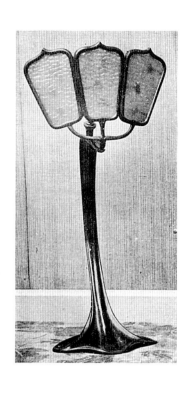

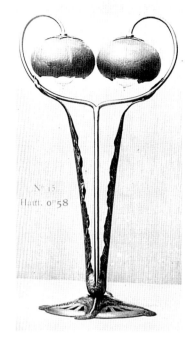

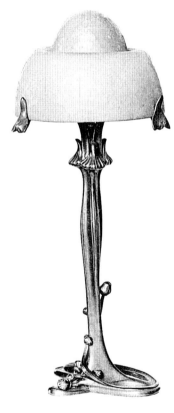

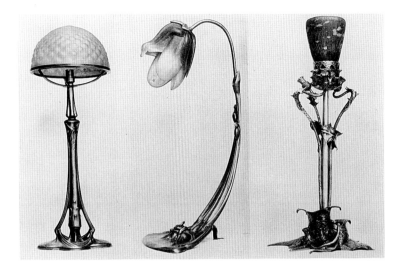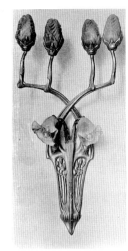

A selection of table-lamps with glass shades by Daum, *c.* 1903; and
(*right*) a wall-sconce with blown-glass shades by Daum, *c.* 1905.

true value of such lamps to the Art Nouveau collector is primarily aesthetic – as a source of ambience lighting.

Examination of the firm's sales catalogues reveals a surprising number of lamp designs with shades made from fabric, rather than glass. In several instances the same design for the bronze base was used in conjunction with both. In the intervening years many of the original fabric-covered shades have disintegrated, or have been discarded, and this has resulted in numerous lamp-bases without shades coming on the market, giving rise to the commonly held, but erroneous, belief among collectors that a corresponding number of *glass* shades must have been broken or lost. A selection of lamps with tasselled and fluted silk shades, designed by Majorelle immediately after World War I, were totally uncharacteristic of his work, and correspondingly gaudy and fussy.[4] Others, again, were embroidered or beaded in what might be best described as the 'high Victorian' style. Perhaps the suspension of the Daum glasshouse's production, caused by wartime hostilities, forced Majorelle to experiment with materials other than glass and with forms that were not glass-oriented. Other examples of lamps with fabric-covered shades, undated (but probably introduced immediately before or after World War I), are less provocative. All Majorelle fabric-covered shades, however, appear dull and nondescript when compared with those which he designed to be produced in glass. To the modern collector, these shades constitute an aberration, and, as such, are totally unrepresentative of what one normally associates with Majorelle's work.

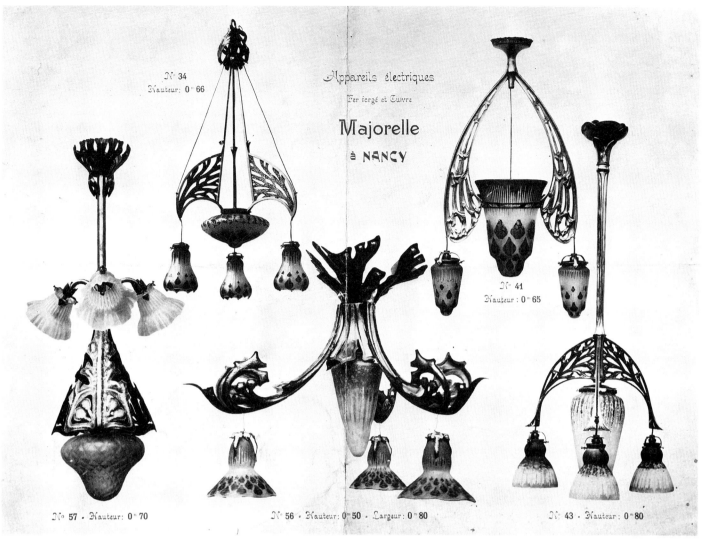

Appareils électriques

Fer forgé et Cuivre

Majorelle

à NANCY

Illustrations from sales catalogues showing (*above*) a selection of ceiling fixtures and (*below*) various table-lamps with Daum glass shades in the form of flowers (water-lily; dandelion; pitcher plant; magnolia).

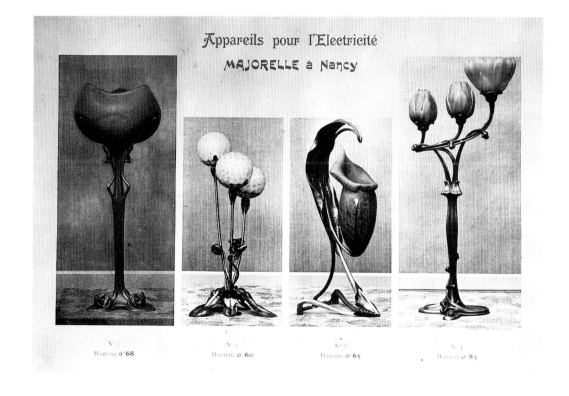

Appareils pour l'Electricité

MAJORELLE à Nancy

Drop-front desk, teak with rosewood veneer and mother-of-pearl inlay, mid-1920s.

7

World War I and later years

THE IMPACT of World War I on the province of Lorraine was nothing short of catastrophic, its proximity to southern Germany exacerbating both the degree of damage to property and the loss of human life. Aerial maps compiled after the cessation of hostilities show the extent to which Nancy and its suburbs had been subjected to regular bombardment from the air (990 bombs dropped from aircraft and 33 from dirigibles) and by artillery fire, the combined effect of which was to reduce more than 600 houses to rubble and cause around 500 casualties.[1] The resultant general disarray and dislocation of services available to the local citizenry, together with the wartime restrictions imposed by the provincial government, had forced Majorelle, like others, to suspend his business activities. Many members of his staff had been mobilized, and this further reduced his capacity to operate.

Several landmark buildings in Nancy were destroyed, including the city's most fashionable department store, the Maison des Magasins Réunis in the Rue du Faubourg Saint-Jean, which was bombed during a night-time air-raid on 15 January 1916. Included in the loss was the store's tea-room furnished by Majorelle, and a large stained-glass window by Jacques Gruber. The announcement in the local press on 12 April that Jean Daum, the master glassworker and eldest son of Auguste Daum, had been killed in combat at the age of thirty-one brought confirmation of a further war-related tragedy that directly affected the remaining members of the now defunct Ecole de Nancy.[2]

The worst blow was still to come, however: the destruction by fire of Majorelle's workshops in the Rue du Vieil-Aître, which occurred later that year on the night of Monday, 20 November.[3] Though reported briefly in four regional newspapers – *L'Eclair de l'Est*, *Le Journal de la Meurthe et des Vosges*, *L'Etoile de l'Est* and *L'Est républicain* – this event was overshadowed by the assassination in the same week of Emperor Franz Josef in Vienna. The death of 'this great criminal', whose ancestors were amongst the last dukes of independent Lorraine, forced local news from all the front pages. In addition, wartime censorship regulations prohibited coverage of any event, such as a fire, which might assist the enemy in determining the success of its bombing missions. The result was a relatively small announcement of a local event which should have been reported as a calamitous loss: the destruction of the workshops of the era's pre-eminent cabinetmaker, whose works had until recently been a source of immense provincial pride. No doubt, in this respect, the decline in popularity of the Art Nouveau movement, combined with the recent demise of the Ecole de Nancy, helped to reduce the event's newsworthiness. (Later, a brief moment of respite from the incessant German onslaught was afforded in late February 1918, when, following the destruction by bombing of its entire printing plant, *L'Est républicain* published a single sheet in which the editor explained the paper's reduced extent as being due to 'a mechanical hitch' ['*un accident aux machines*'].[4] The episode amused the local community immensely, helping momentarily to boost its morale.)

The fire in the Majorelle workshops, the cause of which was accidental, broke out at around 9.30 p.m. in the sculpture studio on the ground floor, and from there it spread rapidly through the premises, its progress accelerated by the large volume of wood on hand, both as stock and in the form of partially made furniture. Alarms were sounded, and the local fire brigade was summoned, but it proved impossible to bring the conflagration under control until 5.00 the next morning. The flames, fanned by the wind from the south-east, also threatened nearby buildings, and placed members of the fire-fighting force at great risk; they received special commendation in the press for their bravery in working the water pumps in the adjoining streets, the Rues Goncourt, Laxou, Palissot and Vannoz.

Two further wartime disasters awaited Majorelle, including the destruction by bombing of his showroom at 20 Rue Saint-Georges in the early evening of 16 October 1917.[5] Also lost in the air-raid, in addition to the building itself, were paintings, furniture and Daum glassware. The canvases, to judge from a contemporary description of the showroom, would typically have included portraits by Emile Friant and Henri Bergé, and Alsatian landscapes by A. Lévy. Perhaps to show its determination not to be thwarted by such aggression, the Majorelle family mounted, within days of the destruction of the showroom, a replacement display in an adjacent shop in the Rue Saint-Georges. As a footnote, almost, to the series of major reversals it had suffered during the war years, the family reported that its branch in Lille had been looted by the German infantry.

During this time of great adversity and upheaval, Majorelle frequently took refuge in Paris, where he was reported to have worked, and housed himself, principally at the Atelier Julian. Here, according to his brother Jules, he honed his painting skills, 'taking up his pencil again, having reverted to being a hard-working pupil, he studied at daily sittings. His sketches – quite elaborate – show that the decorator was also a painter at heart.'[6]

Demobilized after the armistice, Alfred Lévy returned to Nancy to find his old master seated in a corner among the ruins of the workshops in the Rue du Vieil-Aître, 'working at a drawing board propped up on trestles, exhausted and regretting that everything had not been destroyed'.[7] In reality, practically everything had been lost, including all of the correspondence, lists of clients and materials, press cuttings, and records of exhibition entries and awards, in addition to all the furniture sketches, models and moulds which had been preserved by the firm in the course of the fifty-odd years of its existence. Although the full extent of the loss remains unknown, one can assume that as nothing has subsequently become available either in the trade or come directly to local institutions in Nancy, such as the Musée de l'Ecole de Nancy or the Bibliothèque Municipale, from the Majorelle family's few surviving members or from the families of the firm's former employees, the flames must have consumed all,

The remains of the Majorelle showroom at 20 Rue Saint-Georges,
Nancy, after its destruction in an air-raid on 16 October 1917.

or practically all, of the firm's archives. Today we can do no more than speculate about the host of seminal designs and coloured renderings created by Majorelle through the years, including those for the water-lilies and orchids series, that must have been destroyed.

Despite the elimination in this tragic manner of the records and physical evidence of Majorelle's entire career, Lévy reported that he took the loss with equanimity, even perceiving it, in a certain way, as a blessing in disguise. Now that the past had been summarily wiped out by the wartime destruction, he felt that he had no choice but to set about developing a new style for the post-war era (the need to satisfy the changing taste of his clientèle no doubt contributed to this decision). At the age of sixty and doubtless exhausted, like most of Nancy's population, by the protracted conflict, Majorelle would have to summon up extraordinary energy and vision if he was to succeed in regaining his *fin-de-siècle* stature. The return, after the war, of most of his top artisans – including Steiner, Jung, Desgrey, Lognon, Vaubourg and Gatelet – provided him with an auspicious start in meeting the challenge.[8] At the same time, he promoted Alfred Lévy, his long-standing and loyal design assistant, to the position of deputy director.

Reconstruction of the Majorelle workshops, built literally from the ground up, had begun even before the end of the war. Evidence of the new aesthetic in the fields of furniture and interior design, which had germinated prior to 1914 in Paris in the creations of Clément Mère, Paul Iribe and Paul Follot, now began to assert itself at

Double bed with Art Deco floral
panels, early 1920s.

Double bed with matching end-tables,
macassar ebony with ivory trim,
mid-1920s.

the annual Salons, following their reinstatement in 1919. Always a stalwart member, Majorelle participated from 1920 in the Salon d'Automne, and those of the Société des Artistes Décorateurs and the Société des Artistes Français, displaying, in collaboration with the Daum glassworks, a series of his recently conceived glass and wrought-iron vessels. If he had harboured any secret hopes that the hiatus caused by the hostilities might create a feeling of nostalgia for pre-war fashions – specifically the taste of the Belle Epoque – such dreams would have been abrupty dispelled by the exhibits shown by his Salon colleagues. Post-war taste dictated a new, and sharp, linearity, to which was applied a fresh, and more subtle, grammar of surface ornament.

Most critics would neither forget, nor forgive, past excesses. In the General Report, published in 1919, on a French exhibition of decorative arts held in Copenhagen, Emile Bayard struck a note of caution, 'having taken note of the heroic beginnings of modern art, the prolific mistakes of the Ecole de Nancy – with Gallé, with Messrs Majorelle and Prouvé, with Wiener and Martin – this Ecole de Nancy which put ornament before structure, was overfond of clematis, of figured mahogany and inlaid quotations from Rodenbach'. Others were less harsh, however. Indeed, in what was presumably an attempt to identify an evolving national style, one even managed to describe the emerging post-war form of imagery as a *'style nouille géometrisé'*![9]

Majorelle appeared undaunted by the fact that he was now a follower of a new style rather than one of its innovators; he was lauded by Emile Sedeyn in his report on the furniture section at the 1925 Exposition Internationale des Arts Décoratifs et Industriels Modernes, 'Louis Majorelle is not only a precursor, but above all he is one of the artists who pursue – with the greatest competence and application – the study of achieving a contemporary [style of] furniture . . . What he creates stands out and will endure by virtue of its lofty inspiration and of its noble and painstaking workmanship'.[10] Many in a similar position to Majorelle would have quietly bowed out, but he rose to the challenge of the new Modernism, motivated in part, perhaps, by economic necessity. Inevitably, however, the 1920s belonged to a new generation, and the master cabinetmaker was now perceived by many to slip towards obscurity. Pierre Olmer, in *Le Mobilier français d'aujourd'hui (1910–1925)*, provided a summary of Majorelle's predicament, 'Perhaps he did not know how to distance himself quickly enough from some of the mistakes made by the School [of Nancy], which must deserve credit for having courageously led the way in new research. Majorelle's output . . . is a little dated, it is true, but this can be explained on account of its origins . . .'.[11]

The documentary illustrations (pp. 164ff.) include several Majorelle ensembles dating from the years 1920–25. During this period, his furniture was characterized by its massiveness and by the incorporation of the Art Deco imagery adopted at the time by most Parisian furniture designers and cabinetmakers then active in the Faubourg Saint-Antoine. The earlier panels veneered with floral and landscape designs were, as noted, now absent; in their place were large unornamented surfaces in which the rich grain of the wood was allowed to make its own visual impression. Simple perpendicular forms, lightly adorned with small inlaid floral or abstract medallions, represented the new vogue. In this, Majorelle clearly opted for the middle ground, aiming his production at middle-class tastes and purses. His ensembles (shown not just at the Salons but offered directly to the public through his showrooms), are today largely indistinguishable from those of, for example, the leading commercial *ébénistes* active in Paris at the time, such as Eric Bagge, Léon Bouchet, André Fréchet and Lahalle et Lévard. Absent from his output, most nobably, was a range of spectacular works of the kind which had punctuated his pre-war production, specifically the ormolu-mounted series. In the absence of such highlights, his 1920s designs are difficult to distinguish from those of his contemporaries. The 'Majorellisme' which had earlier electrified his *fin-de-siècle* audience was gone.

The evolution of Majorelle's style can be traced in his choice of materials. His early preference for darker woods – mahogany, purpleheart, rosewood – remained, joined in the 1920s by macassar ebony and palisander. To these, ivory trim was introduced as a contrasting decorative accent, either to trace the contours of a piece of furniture or to form cross-hatched or chequered panelling.

Alfred Lévy's collaboration was first listed formally at the 1920 Salon d'Automne when his name was given in connection with a display cabinet featuring wrought-iron mounts. The following year came a dining-room ensemble in macassar ebony and amaranth. The critic for *Art et décoration* found it to have a solid and logical opulence, despite its monumentality. The latter comment was predictable, for Majorelle had suffered such criticism intermittently for thirty years. In 1923, Gaston Varenne touched on the issue from a slightly different viewpoint, writing in *Art et décoration* that the firm designed furniture 'for men only'.[12]

By 1924, the illness which had debilitated him for several years incapacitated Majorelle just at the point when the firm was preparing its display for the following year's Exposition Internationale des Arts Décoratifs et Industriels Modernes. He retired to his son's home in Marrakech, a villa with great landscaped gardens filled with exotic flora and fountains. Here he convalesced, having entrusted Lévy with supervising the manufacture of the firm's furnishings, and returned to France some time before the opening of the Exposition.

Majorelle was appointed a member of the Jury for Class 7 (furniture and ensembles), and was promoted to Officier de la Légion d'Honneur. Because of his official involvement as a juror, the two ensembles he submitted were exhibited *hors concours*. The Exposition of 1925 must have brought painful memories to the aging Majorelle. Gone were the fanfare and limelight accorded the splendid Art Nouveau bedroom suite he had exhibited twenty-five years earlier, in their place virtual obscurity among the era's new generation of cabinetmakers. Absent, too, were the bulk of his old Ecole de Nancy cohorts: Gallé, Prouvé, Vallin and Gauthier. Jacques Gruber had survived, but solely as a stained-glass artist. The Daum glassworks, after several close brushes with bankruptcy in the second decade of the century, had responded vigorously to the 1920s aesthetic, and was Lorraine's proudest exhibitor, unlike the ailing Gallé Cristallerie, whose by now outmoded glassware was passed over by the novelty-seeking critics. The Exposition did, however, provide Majorelle

Suite of library furniture with carved decoration and wrought-iron
mounts, mid-1920s.

Cabinet/vitrine, mid-1920s.

with a wistful opportunity to recall the Ecole de Nancy's supremacy a quarter of a
century earlier. In an article entitled 'Nancy, la Région Lorraine', written on the
occasion of the XVIIIth Congress of Medicine held at the time of the Exposition, he
reminisced on former glories: 'The participation of the workshops of Lorraine in the
1900 Exposition and the well-deserved successes they achieved there have given our
region an enhanced position in the furniture-making industry: the cabinetmakers
Gallé, Vallin and Majorelle came out on top. Nancy was at the forefront of a
movement which was no longer just imitating whatever was produced in the
Faubourg Saint-Antoine in Paris; our output had a modern feel which became firmly
established: it found its final approval in the Exposition des Arts Décoratifs
Modernes of 1925. I am proud to say that Lorraine was the starting point for this
great artistic expression, for here the first works possessing modern characteristics
date from thirty years ago. We are entitled to feel proud of this.'[13]

Majorelle died on 15 January 1926, showing until the end great stoicism and
bravery in the face of an undiagnosed illness. At the same time his son Jacques'
sickness prevented him from travelling from his home in Marrakech in order to be at
his father's bedside in Nancy, thus making the family's loss all the more painful.

* * *

Retrospective exhibitions at both major annual Parisian Salons paid tribute to
Lorraine's master cabinetmaker. The first, at the Salon d'Automne of 1926,
displayed a mahogany and locustwood desk and chair *aux nénuphars*, first shown at

157

the 1900 Exposition Universelle, alongside a buffet in amaranth, macassar ebony and American walnut from the 1922 Salon d'Automne. The contrast between total luxuriance and total constraint, the opposing lodestars of the Art Nouveau and Art Deco philosophies, was made especially significant when viewed in the work of a single *ébéniste*. The Salon des Artistes Décorateurs held a similar retrospective the following year: turn-of-the-century examples of designs *aux orchidées* and *aux algues* were displayed with one of Majorelle's last works, dating from 1925, a smoking room in coralwood, which he had designed in collaboration with Lévy, Janin (stained-glass windows) and Francin (carpets).[14]

After 1926 Les Ateliers Majorelle continued, under Alfred Lévy's directorship, to exhibit at the Paris Salons and in national and international exhibitions. In 1928, for example, it participated in an exhibition in Athens, in 1929 in the third of a series entitled La Décoration Française Contemporaine in Paris, and, in 1930, in Madrid. Lévy was joined at this time by Pierre Majorelle, the son of Louis' youngest brother, Pierre, and a graduate of both the Ecole des Beaux-Arts and the Ecole Boulle, who had earlier gained practical experience in the family workshops in the Rue du Vieil-Aître. Pierre was listed as an interior decorator and Lévy's collaborator in an office interior displayed at the 1930 Salon d'Automne, for which Paul Colin (paintings), Guénot (sculpture), Dunand (vases), Décor et Luminière (lamps) and Lehucher (window shades) were also credited in the exhibition catalogue. The ensemble appeared strangely impersonal and stark, lacking much of the fullness and warmth that had been the hallmark of Majorelle interiors for so many years. This signified the firm's gradual movement away from a total dependency on wood, and towards the use of metal and glass, an approach shared by most cabinetmakers at the start of the new decade. The firm's furniture was still made primarily in wood – walnut, sycamore, macassar ebony, Cuban mahogany, palisander, chickweed and other varieties – but wider use was made now of polished steel, etched glass and crystal for components such as shelves, brackets and feet. This new breakdown corresponded to designs introduced by Michel Dufet, Jules Leleu, Paul Follot, and Lucie Holt le Son at the same Salons (1930–33). The influence of the Union des Artistes Modernes (U.A.M.), proponents of hard-edged metallic modernism who had united officially in 1929, was to be seen even amongst the more conservative members of the furniture-making industry.

A special challenge was presented by the 1931 Exposition Coloniale in Paris, which attracted a full complement of French designers and manufacturers. The Majorelle ensembles – a library and office – were handsome enough, but were lacking in personality and individualism, which were a matter for concern for several critics. Among them was Yvanhoë Rambosson who, in a review of the firm's production published in *Mobilier et décoration* in 1933, noted that, while the firm's attempt to maintain a sense of continuity was admirable, the inevitable danger in this was sterility and anonymity.[15]

Further tragedy struck the family and the firm in 1933 and 1934: first came the premature death on 9 February 1933 of Pierre Majorelle, at the age of 29: and, the next year, that of Jules Majorelle. M. Destrez, the latter's son-in-law, was placed in

Views of the retrospective exhibition of furniture by Majorelle at
the Salon d'Automne, 1926. In the upper illustration several pieces
originally shown at the 1900 Exposition Universelle can be seen;
these include the bedroom suite and other items *aux orchidées*. The
lower photograph shows various models produced after World
War I.

charge of the firm's commercial affairs. By 1936, Paul Beucher, another graduate of the Ecole Boulle, and a former assistant to Jacques-Emile Ruhlmann, likewise joined, his role being to assist Lévy in decorating and in technical matters.[16] Business was clearly sound, if not expanding. An article in *Le Pays lorrain* in 1937 listed a Majorelle workshop in Lyons, and salesrooms in Nancy and Paris, as well as overseas in Algiers and Oran. Commissions were increasingly for large public or corporate interiors, such as conference rooms, offices and libraries, for a client list that included local Chambers of Commerce, city halls and universities. Other notable sources of commissions were industrial concerns such as the Mines de Lens, the Hauts Fourneaux de Pont à Mousson and the Aciéres de Longwy, as well as interiors for the University of Nancy, various restaurants, banks and ocean liners.[17]

A final international showcase of note awaited the firm: the Exposition Internationale des Arts et Techniques Appliqués à la Vie Moderne, held in Paris in 1937. On this occasion interiors in palisander, ash, walnut, sycamore, mahogany and lemonwood were created for the firm's displays in the Pavillon des Artistes Décorateurs and the Pavillon de la Lorraine. Collaborators included, in particular, Etienne Cournault, also from Nancy, who had provided the firm throughout the 1930s with a delightful, and highly distinctive, selection of engraved and painted glass panels for incorporation into large pieces of furniture. As it had done earlier, the Daum glassworks continued to design the glassware for the Majorelle interiors. Further credit was given also to Mme Catherine J. Moreillon of Epinal (fabrics), Genet et Michon (lighting), Hutchinson (carpets), Bassino (etched glass), and Jean Prouvé (a metal door); the last mentioned later emerged as a leading light among French furniture designers of the 1940s and 1950s.

After World War II, the firm continued to operate for ten years, before closing voluntarily, and quietly. It had been exactly a century since Auguste Majorelle had opened his modest shop and a ceramic-decorating business in Toul, a full half of which had been spent by the firm in the shadow of its spectacular triumphs at the Exposition Universelle of 1900. Like the family businesses of Gallé and Vallin, which had lingered on for too long after the creative flame of their founders had been extinguished, the time had come for the curtain to be lowered on that of the Majorelles.

Alfred Lévy standing beside one of his bookcases designed in the late 1920s.

CONTEMPORARY DOCUMENTS

Works illustrated in sales catalogues,
magazines and other publications

THIS DOCUMENTARY APPENDIX consists of illustrations taken from the Majorelle firm's sales catalogues and from miscellaneous publications dating from the same period. The firm published a series of catalogues, material from four of which has been incorporated here. The largest of these, which was reprinted in the early 1980s, has until now been the primary reference source for Majorelle's furniture production. The others, smaller and in each case including a selection of illustrations that also featured in the large catalogue, were in one instance aimed specifically at a wealthy clientèle, and in the other two at middle-income buyers.

None of the sales catalogues is dated, hence it is impossible to determine the precise year in which each furniture design was introduced. Although it has generally been assumed that the largest catalogue was published c. 1910, this date can now be shown to be incorrect, for certain items included in it, such as Majorelle's edition of *verreries ferronnées* (blown-glass vases, bowls and lampshades in wrought-iron armatures), were in fact conceived during World War I, and only introduced at the Paris Salons immediately thereafter. The catalogue was therefore probably published c. 1920/21, this dating being substantiated further by the inclusion of some items of furniture in a distinctly 'Art Deco' style. The other three catalogues appear to date from roughly the same period, if not slightly later. Also included here are illustrations of Majorelle ensembles originally published in relatively obscure regional journals, such as the *Bulletin des sociétés artistiques de l'Est* and the *Revue lorraine illustrée*, and photographs showing Majorelle's displays at the annual Salons, particularly those held in Paris.

The contemporary documents reveal several important aspects of Majorelle's business, especially the degree to which it was committed to industrialized methods, producing limited editions of machine-made furniture. By far the largest part of its output consisted of medium-priced furnishings aimed at the middle and upper-middle classes. In fact, most of the examples shown include only a modicum of decoration, such as lightly carved mouldings and/or undistinguished marquetry panels. Many other pieces are nondescript and would today be unidentifiable as the work of Majorelle, were it not for the evidence provided by their inclusion in the firm's catalogues (pieces such as these frequently left the studios unsigned). Most of these items show a light Art Nouveau influence in their shape and floral ornamentation, while others are distinctly provincial in feeling. Some, even, are more accurately classified as 'rustic', or as 'Arts and Crafts'. Two illustrations (that is, the

162

photographs, if not the furniture), dating from 1906 (ills. 76, 77), show ensembles in Louis XVI style which, in terms of their fidelity to eighteenth-century design, rival anything manufactured from the 1880s in Paris by period-revival cabinetmakers. There remains, finally, a selection of 'Art Deco' pieces and interiors, such as the 'Ginette' and 'Les Roses' models (ills. 113–115), which appear to date from the start of the 1920s. Perpendicular in shape, with veneered panels or medallions of stylized bouquets or baskets of flowers, these are generally interchangeable with the creations of several Parisian furniture designers at the time, for example, Maurice Dufrène (in his role as artistic director of La Maîtrise, the design studio for the Galeries Lafayette department store, Eric Bagge, Lahalle et Lévard, and Charlotte Chaucet-Guillère (artistic director of Primavera, the design studio of the Printemps department store).

From the evidence presented here it becomes clear that Majorelle's masterpieces, including the water-lily and orchid series, were in fact subsidized by the large volume of average-quality commercial pieces manufactured by the firm. As in the case of Gallé, it was his commercial output that effectively underpinned the majestic creations shown to the world at national and international exhibitions. Undoubtedly, much of the average production would not have been a source of pride for Majorelle or his staff, but the profits from such sales did permit the creation of those *de luxe* works for which Majorelle is now renowned.

Another feature of interest within the appendix is the wide variety of designs for light-fixtures which Majorelle produced either on his own (with fabric-covered shades), or in collaboration with the Daum glassworks. Concerning the latter, many table models incorporate shades and bases made of glass; i.e., *only* the mount was of metal and therefore by Majorelle. The close business relationship between the two firms no doubt made it possible for Majorelle to promote these lamps in his catalogues as his own, rather than as works by Daum.

The illustrations of completed interiors reveal a preoccupation with compact, even cluttered, life-styles typical of the Victorian era. The congested appearance of many of Majorelle's room settings results in part from his use of painted wall-panels and friezes which, in turn, were sometimes used in conjunction with decorative stained-glass windows. Built-in furniture units added to the appearance of comfort and affluence, as did the inclusion of painted panels (*trumeaux*) placed above the mirrors that surmounted Majorelle's fireplaces. Sadly, the black-and-white illustrations from the period cannot reveal the overall colour-schemes of these interiors. Surviving swatches of wall and lampshade fabrics and upholstered chair covers do, however, provide a good idea of Majorelle's original palette of earth tones, even though they are now invariably faded.

Furniture and interiors, c. 1900–1908

1 Dining-room suite.

2, 3 Domestic interiors.

4 General view of salon.

5 Corner of a salon with fitted furniture.

6 Dining-room suite with carved floral decoration.

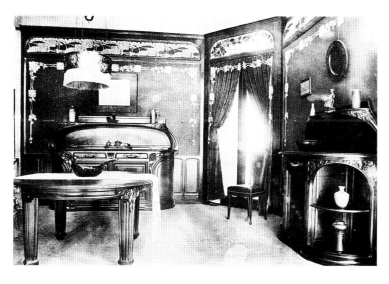

7, 8 Interior of the Jansen showroom, Paris, designed by Sauvage et Sarazin and with furniture by Majorelle, 1902.

9 Artist's quarters designed by Sauvage et Sarazin, with seating by Majorelle.

10 Corner of a salon.

11 Grand piano and furniture for a music salon.

12 Corner of a boudoir.

167

13–15 Salon-library (*left*), study furniture (*below left*) and chimneypiece (*below*), all with gilt-bronze mounts.

16 Bedroom suite with carved decoration
and gilt-bronze mounts.

The orchid ('Orchidée') as decorative motif

17, 18 Salon and study furniture with gilt-bronze mounts.

19, 20 Study interior with furniture in amaranth with gilt-bronze mounts.

Clematis ('Clématites') as decorative motif

21–24 Furniture for salons (*right and below*) and bedrooms (*bottom*), all with carved decoration.

The fern ('Fougère') as decorative motif

25–27 Salon furniture and a bedroom suite with carved decoration.

Seaweed ('Les Algues') as decorative motif

28–31 Bedroom suite (model no. 305), chimneypiece, dining-room suite (model no. 515) and another bedroom suite, all with carved decoration.

32–34 Study furniture *aux algues*.

Vine decoration

35–39 Variant forms of 'La Vigne' dining-room furniture, one (*left*) featuring rounded corners.

40–42 Dining-room furniture with carved decoration: (*top*) 'Viorne' (viburnum); (*centre*) 'Céphataria'; (*below*) 'Lulu'.

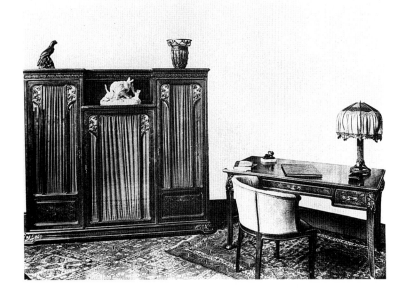

43, 44 Study furniture 'Junko'; for the table-lamp on the left in the lower illustration, see colour plate 118.

45 Salon furniture 'Attacia', with (*centre*) *étagère* 'La Mer'.

46 Salon furniture 'Ombelles' (umbels).

47 Bedroom suite 'Les Lilas' (lilacs).

48 Bedroom suite 'Passiflores'
(passionflowers), model no. 348.

49, 51, 53 (*left-hand column*)
Chimneypiece and dining-room suites
'Chicorée' (*bottom*: model no. 320).

50, 52, 54 (*right-hand column*)
Chimneypiece and dining-room suites 'Les
Blés' with carved decoration representing
ears of wheat.

55–57 Bedroom suites: (*top and centre*) with ornate mouldings ('moulurations ornées'; *top*, model no. 253); and (*bottom*) in modern style, lacquered white and pale lilac.

58–61 Groups of study furniture 'Les Pins' with carved pine-cone decoration.

62, 63 Salon and boudoir furniture
'Aubépine' (hawthorn).

64 Salon furniture 'Olga' (model no. 323)
and matching buffet-vitrine (model no.
353).

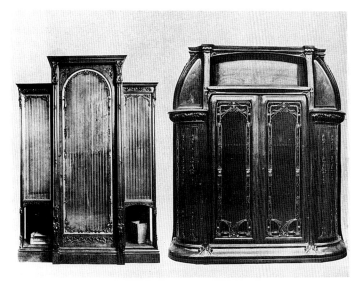 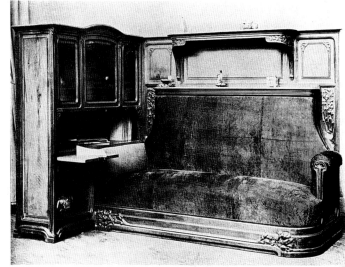

65 Cabinet 'Sagittaires' (arrowheads) and
bookcase 'Pavillon de Marsan'.

66 Corner unit including divan and
bookcase

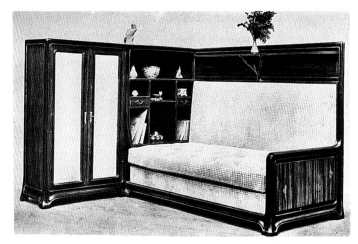

67–70 Corner and wall units, each with
divan

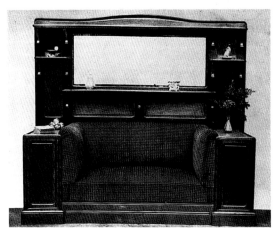

71 Salon fireplace

72 Study interior

73 Fireplace and flanking display cabinets for silver 'Les Capucines' (nasturtiums).

75 Buffet 'Noisetier' (hazel tree).

74 Salon fireplace and corner light-fixture.

76, 77 Bedroom suite in mahogany with
gilt-bronze mounts and salon furniture,
both in Louis XVI style, 1906.

80 Bedroom furniture 'Les Papillons' (butterflies), model no. 426.

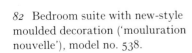

81 Bedroom furniture with moulded decoration ('à moulurations'), model no. 348 *bis*.

82 Bedroom suite with new-style moulded decoration ('mouluration nouvelle'), model no. 538.

83 Bedroom suite 'Pirouettes', model no. 512.

84 Bedroom suite 'Spill', model no. 539.

85 Bedroom suite 'I2B', model no. 543.

86 Dining-room furniture 'Tomates',
model no. 321.

87 Dining-room furniture 'Les Algues'
(seaweed), model no. 335.

88 Dining-room furniture 'Junko', model
no. 552.

89 Dining-room furniture 'Houblons'
(hops), model 324.

90 Dining-room furniture 'Houblons'
(hops).

91 Dining-room furniture 'Houblons'
(hops), model no. 540.

92 Dining-room furniture 'Pois fleurs',
model no. 560.

93 Dining-room furniture 'Les Blés' (ears of wheat), model no. 544.

94 Dining-room furniture 'Les Blés', small version.

95 Dining-room furniture 'Les Pommes' (apples).

96 Dining-room furniture 'Les Courges' (marrow/squash flowers).

97 Dining-room furniture 'Cordifeuilles'.

98 Dining-room furniture.

99 Dining-room furniture.

100 Study furniture 'Sceau de Salomon'
(Solomon's seal), model no. 411.

101 Study furniture 'Hémisphères'.

102 Study furniture, model no. 425.

103 Study furniture 'Attacia', model no. 559.

104 Study furniture.

105 Study furniture, 'Flore Marine' (marine flora), model no. 433.

195

106 Cabinets and shelf unit, from left to right model nos. 473, 474, 489.

107 Bedroom furniture, model no. 156.

108 Study furniture 'Cardère' (teasel), model no. 327.

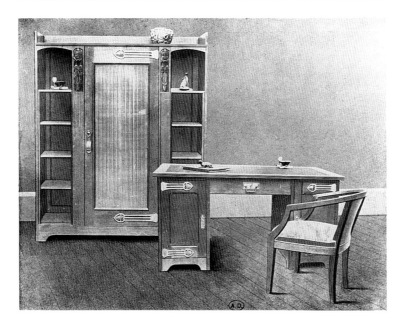

Furniture, 1919 and later

109 Dining-room furniture 'Symphorine',
model no. 408.

110 Study furniture 'Alain', model no.
410.

111 Bedroom furniture 'Ginette', model
no. 424.

112 Dining-room furniture 'Les Roses', model no. 456.

113–115 Bedroom furniture 'Les Roses': (*above*) model nos. 349 and 349 *bis*, the latter with matching double bed (not shown).

116 Study furniture.

117 Study furniture 'Médaillon', model no. 462.

118 Salon cabinets, model nos. 438, 400.

199

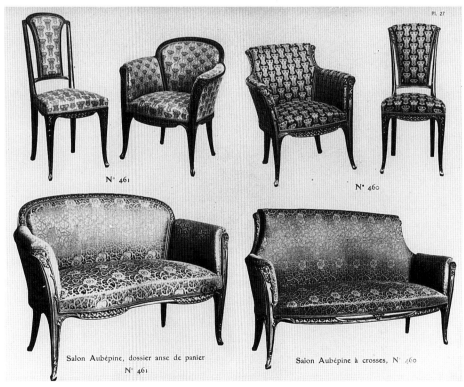

N° 461

N° 460

Salon Aubépine, dossier anse de panier
N° 461

Salon Aubépine à crosses, N° 460

200

Miscellaneous pieces and groups of furniture

119   Hall furniture.

120   Salon seating 'Aubépine' (hawthorn), model nos. 461 (*left*) and 460 (*right*).

121–123   Salon furniture.

N° 436

N° 437

N° 435

N° 421

N° 431

125–127 Salon furniture.

124 Two pedestal tables, c. 1910.

128–130 Salon furniture.

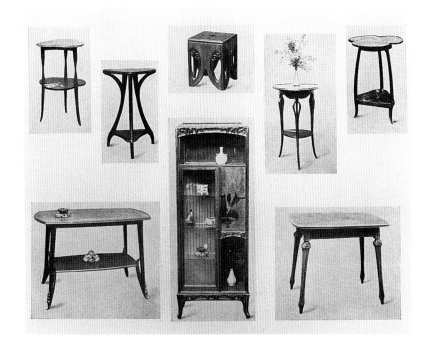

131–133 Salon furniture.

134–136 Salon furniture.

137–139 Salon furniture.

 *140* Salon furniture.

141 Cabinet illustrated in an
advertisement for the Majorelle firm in
Les Echos des industries d'art, June 1926.

142 Dressing tables.

143 Lady's writing desk, model no. 248.

144 *Guéridon*, model no. 250, and tea table, model no. 249.

Metalwork

145 Wrought-iron banisters with botanical motifs.

146 Two wrought-iron tripods exhibited at the Salon de la Société des Artistes Décorateurs, Paris, 1908.

147 Wrought-iron and bronze doors: (*left*) 'Monnaie-du-pape' (satin-pods); (*right*) 'Erable' (maple).

148 Wrought-iron entrance gates and glazed *marquise*, Chambre de Commerce et d'Industrie, Nancy, 1908; cf. colour plate 100.

149, 150 Groups of *verreries ferronnées*:
vases and bowls combining metal
armatures by Majorelle and blown glass
by Daum Frères.

Lighting

151–153 Groups of table-lamps and
light-fixtures.

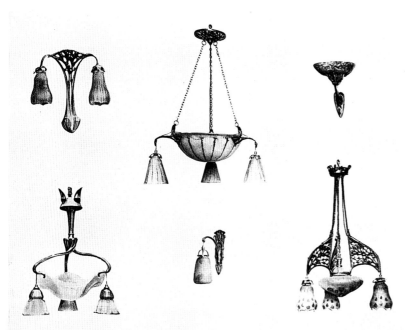

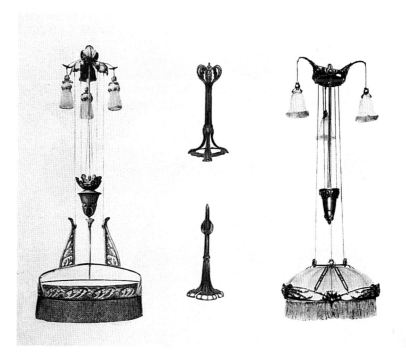

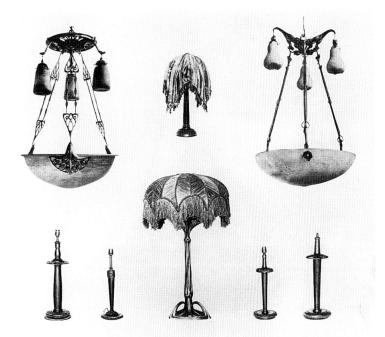

154–156 Groups of table-lamps, light-fixtures and standard lamps.

Lampadaire Poincaré

157–159 Groups of table-lamps and
light-fixtures.

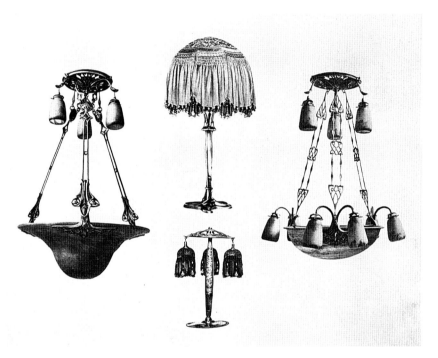

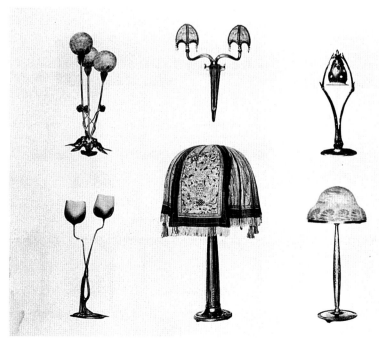

Pl. 1

N° 1

N° 2

N° 3

N° 4

N° 5

N° 6

N° 4

160–162 Groups of table-lamps.

Pl. 2

N° 7

N° 8

N° 9

N° 10

N° 11

N° 12

N° 13

N° 14

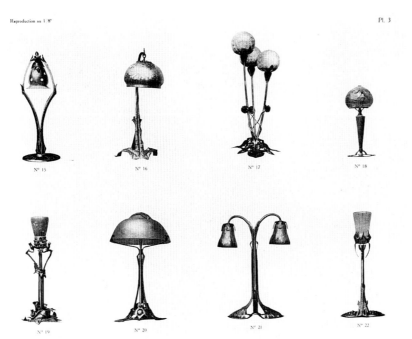

Pl. 3

N° 15

N° 16

N° 17

N° 18

N° 19

N° 20

N° 21

N° 22

Pl. 4

163–165 Groups of table-lamps and light-fixtures.

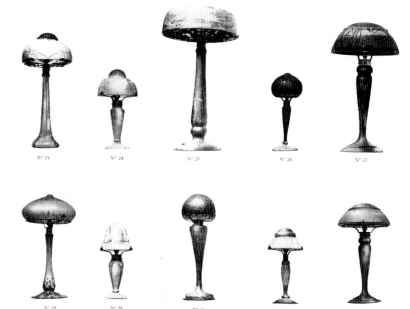

N° 23   N° 24   N° 25   N° 26   N° 27

N° 28   N° 29   N° 40   N° 31   N° 32

Pl. 5

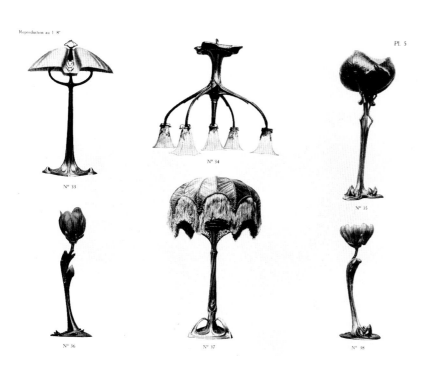

N° 33

N° 34

N° 35

N° 36   N° 37   N° 38

Pl. 6

N° 40

N° 41

N° 42   N° 43

Pl. 7

N° 44

N° 46

N° 45

166–168 Groups of light-fixtures.

Pl. 8

N° 48

N° 49

N° 50

N° 51

N° 52

N° 53

Pl. 9

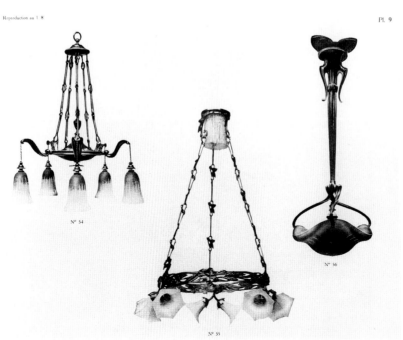

N° 54

N° 55

N° 56

169–171 Groups of light-fixtures.

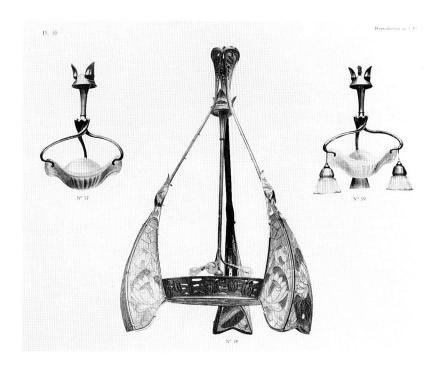

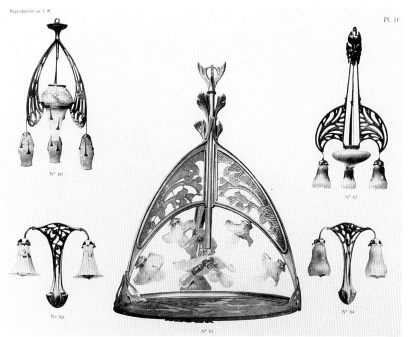

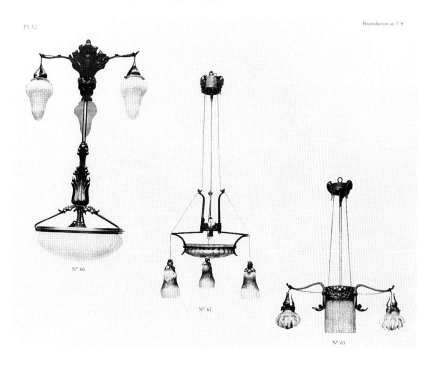

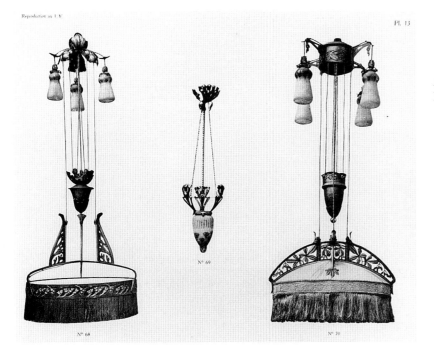

N° 68   N° 69   N° 70

172–174 Groups of table-lamps and light-fixtures.

Pl. 14   Reproduction au 1/8°

N° 71   N° 74

N° 75   N° 72   N° 76

N° 77   N° 79

N° 80   N° 78   N° 80

Notes on the text

Introduction

1. Despite the revival of interest in the Art Nouveau movement fully twenty years ago, when biographers, such as Philippe Garner, began their research on Emile Gallé and his colleagues in the Ecole de Nancy, no substantive information on Majorelle has come to light.
2. Of immense value in this respect is a 158-page file, entitled 'Le Fonds Ancien sur l'Art Nouveau', compiled by the staff of the Municipal Library in Nancy, which chronicles events, exhibitions, publications, lectures etc. that relate to the Ecole de Nancy and its individual members.
3. Jules Majorelle *et al.*, *Louis Majorelle* (1927), p. 6.
4. *Ibid.*, p. 29.
5. An information plaque in the Musée de l'Ecole de Nancy credits the Parisian architect and interior designer Tony Selmersheim (1871–1971) with the original concept from which Majorelle developed the general principles of his furniture design. Selmersheim's *coiffeuse*, shown at the 1898 Salons, and published in the same year in *Art et décoration* (which Majorelle would certainly have read), incorporated the basic shapes which Majorelle drew on in developing his own distinctive style.

1. *Auguste Majorelle and the family firm*

1. The Rue Godron is today nearer to the centre of Nancy than to its extremity. In the 1860s, the city's population was less than 50,000; this figure had doubled by 1900 as the region's iron-ore deposits were progressively developed.
2. Jules Majorelle, in his 1927 biography of Louis (see Introduction, note 3), recorded that there were eight children. However, in the 'Faire-part' files (announcements of births, marriages and deaths on printed cards) in the Municipal Library in Nancy, there is no record of an eighth child. Only seven are recorded there, and one – Achille – had apparently died by 1912.
3. I am indebted to Mlle Marie-Claire Mangin, of the Municipal Library, Nancy, for information from the library's 'Faire-part' files.
4. Several decorative arts exhibitions held in Nancy during this period were reviewed by Edmond de Goncourt and Roger Marx, who later established themselves as Lorraine's foremost art critics and connoisseurs.

5. Surviving biographical information on Auguste Majorelle is concise and consistent. See, for example, 'Majorelle', *L'Information*, Supplément industriel sur la Lorraine, Paris, 1923, p. 53; and Françoise-Thérèse Charpentier, *Art Nouveau L'Ecole de Nancy* (1987), pp. 180–3, 190–3.
6. See Edgard Auguin, *Impressions et Souvenirs: 1875 Exposition de Nancy* (Nancy, 1875), p. 50.
7. Information provided in Majorelle's entry in the catalogue of the 1899 Salon of the Société des Artistes Français, Paris; 'Majorelle né à Toul (Meurthe-et-Moselle), élève de M. Larcher et Devilly à Nancy . . .'. Louis-Théodore Devilly (1818–86) was a noted local teacher of art; M. Larcher's credentials are not known.

2. *Louis Majorelle: the early years, 1880–1899*

1. No record exists of Majorelle's tutelage under Millet if, in fact, a formal course of instruction existed. Common to many entries in Bénézit, and in other dictionaries that cover this period of French art, the relationship between master and student was undefined beyond the vague but (for the student) impressive reference to 'tutelage'. Whether this was personal instruction, or as a member of a large class, or, even, if it implied only that the student had permission to visit the master's *atelier* to view him and his staff working, is mostly unrecorded. In Millet's case, it is unlikely that a painter of such renown would have allocated much time to teach a novice such as Majorelle.
2. Alfred Lévy, 'Louis Majorelle: artiste décorateur, maître ébéniste, Nancy, 1859–1926', *Prestige*, Nancy, no. 6, 1959, p. 3.
3. See Roselyne Bouvier, *La Villa Majorelle* (Nancy, n.d.), note 1.
4. Roger Marx, *L'Art à Nancy en 1882: avec une lettre d'Alexandre Hepp . . .* (Nancy, 1883), pp. 101–8.
5. During the late 1870s and 1880s numerous articles were published attesting to Gallé's prominence as a ceramic and glass artist. See, for example, Jules Henrivaux, *Le Verre et le cristal* (Paris, 1886). Gallé himself published several articles on his glass-making techniques, and these brought him further recognition.
6. Hokkai (1850–1931) arrived in Nancy in 1885,

where he attended the city's school of forestry as a foreign student.
7. Charles de Méixmoron de Dombasle, *Le Paysage d'après Nature* (Nancy, 1890); P. Plauszewski, *La Plante ornementale: branches et feuillages* (Paris, c. 1890), and *Plantes et fleurs décoratives de plein air: Printemps* (Paris, c. 1890).
8. Illustrated in *Art et industrie* (Nancy), July–December 1909, unpaginated.
9. Roger Marx, 'La Décoration et l'art industriel à l'Exposition Universelle de 1889', paper delivered at the Congress of the Société Centrale des Architectes Français, 17 June 1890.
10. See *Exposition d'art décoratif et industriel lorrain*, exhibition catalogue, Salle Poirel, Nancy, June–July 1894: Majorelle's display was listed under Nos. 590–601.
11. *Ibid.*; Majorelle's Louis XV pieces included a 'Bahut style Louis XV, bois sculpté et doré, panneaux vernis Martin' (No. 599).
12. The names of Majorelle's workers were listed frequently in the catalogue entries of his works shown at important exhibitions, e.g. those of the Ecole de Nancy in Paris in 1903; in Nancy in 1904; and in Strasbourg in 1908.

3. *The Exposition Universelle (1900) and the fruits of success*

1. See, for example, G. M. Jacques, 'Le Meuble français à l'Exposition', *L'Art décoratif*, July 1900, p. 147.
2. Majorelle exhibited two cabinets, entitled 'La Cascade' and 'Les Baigneuses' respectively, at the 1898 and 1899 Salons of the Société des Artistes Français in Paris; in their forms and complex workmanship these can in retrospect be considered to have anticipated his success at the 1900 Exposition Universelle. Clearly well received by the public and/or critics, the same models (with slight changes) were later reintroduced by Majorelle at the Salons after 1900.
3. For illustrations of the water-lily desk and bookcase displayed at the 1900 Exposition, see Théodore Lambert, *Meubles de style moderne Exposition Universelle de 1900* (Paris n.d.), pl. 1, no. 1, and pl. 3, no. 4; see also *L'Art décoratif*, July 1900, pp. 142, 143.
4. Théodore Lambert, *op. cit.*, pl. 1, nos. 2 and 4; pl. 2, nos. 1–3.
5. *L'Art décoratif*, July 1900, pp. 142–3.

6. *Ibid.*, p. 147.

7. *L'Art décoratif*, October 1901, p. 16.

8. Critics at the 1900 Exposition referred to Gallé's large cabinet as an 'églantier' (eglantine). Its official name, published by Gallé in his report on his works at the Exposition, was 'La Blanche Vigne'. For illustrations of it, see *La Lorraine artiste*, 1900, p. 97; *La Décoration et les industries d'art à l'Exposition de 1900*, 1900, p. 54; and Alastair Duncan, *Art Nouveau Furniture* (London and New York, 1982), pl. 58.

9. Raoul Aubry *et al.*, 'Documents sur l'art industriel au vingtième siècle', La Maison Moderne, Paris, 1901, unpaginated.

10. Octave Gerdeil, *L'Art décoratif*, October 1901, p. 25.

11. *Ibid.*, pp. 19–20.

12. The term 'courbaril' is not generally used by cabinetmakers today, and there is no record of precisely which wood it referred to at the turn of the century. A plaque in the Musée de l'Ecole de Nancy describes it as an 'essence d'Afrique équatoriale' ('species from equatorial Africa').

13. Majorelle designed many complete ensembles around these flora. See the Contemporary Documents, pp. 161ff., for illustrations.

14. Five examples of such pianos are known to exist that incorporate one of the two decorative friezes specially designed by Victor Prouvé; they were produced by Majorelle between 1903 and 1905. One, with a frieze inspired by a story by Richepin, and entitled 'Chanson de l'Homme au Sable', was donated by Majorelle in 1919 to the Musée des Arts Décoratifs, Paris. Of the remaining four examples, which are based on the legend of 'La Mort du Cygne', one is in the collections of the Musée de l'Ecole de Nancy (gift of J.B.E. Corbin, 1935), and three are in private collections (two in the United States, and one in Japan). A sixth example, lacking Prouvé's decorative frieze, was sold at Sotheby's, New York, in 1985; see *Important Art Nouveau and Art Deco*, auction catalogue no. 5327 ('Marqueterie'), 17 and 18 May 1985, lot 496 (illustrated).

15. For illustrations of exceptional works produced by Majorelle between 1900 and 1910, see the various magazines which reviewed modern decorative arts in France during this period. In Paris, these included *L'Art décoratif*, *Art et décoration* and *La Revue des arts décoratifs*; in Nancy, *Le Bulletin des sociétés artistiques de l'Est*, *La Revue lorraine illustrée*, *Art et industrie*, *La Lorraine artiste* and *L'Art en Lorraine*.

16. Two catalogues were published on the occasion of the Ecole de Nancy's exhibition at the Pavillon de Marsan in Paris. These were: *Exposition de l'Alliance Provinciale des Industries d'Art, l'Ecole de Nancy*, exhibition catalogue, Union Centrale des Arts Décoratifs, Paris, March 1903; and *L'Exposition de l'Ecole de Nancy à Paris* (Armand Guermet, Librairie d'Art Décoratif), Paris, 1903. Both included illustrations and a list of the objects shown by each participant.

17. *L'Exposition d'Art Décoratif, Ecole de Nancy*, exhibition catalogue, the Société des Amis des Arts, Salle Poirel, Nancy, 1904. Majorelle's exhibits were listed in the catalogue as Nos. 190–213.

18. For comments on Majorelle's display, see *Exposition Internationale de Saint-Louis, USA, 1904*, Section française, Rapport général, Henry-Edouard Hammelle *et al.* (Vermot, Paris, 1911[?]), 2 vols., pp. 435ff., 490.

19. For a list of the pieces in Majorelle's display (Nos. 150–155), see *Exposition d'art décoratif de l'Ecole de Nancy*, exhibition catalogue published by the Société des Amis des Arts de Strasbourg, Palais de Rohan, 7 March–26 April 1908.

20. Vallin's pavilion is illustrated in Françoise-Thérèse Charpentier, 'L'Ecole de Nancy et le renouveau de l'art décoratif en France', *Médecine de France*, no. 154, July 1964, p. 32. See also Françoise-Thérèse Charpentier, *Art Nouveau L'Ecole de Nancy* (1987), p. 135.

21. See *Nancy illustré: mondain, thermal, littéraire, artistique, sportif* (Organe officiel de la Cie Fermière des Thermes de la Ville de Nancy), January 1913, vol. 1, pp. 11–14.

22. For biographical information on Jacques Majorelle, see Félix Marcilhac, *La Vie et l'œuvre de Jacques Majorelle* (ACR Edition, Paris), 1988.

23. Mlle Marie-Claire Mangin, of the Municipal Library, Nancy, kindly provided the biographical information on the Majorelle family derived from marriage and death notices of the period.

24. Jules Majorelle *et al.*, *Louis Majorelle*, op. cit., p. 12.

4. *The Villa Majorelle*

1. Gabriel Mourey, 'Une Villa moderne', *L'Illustration*, 12 April 1902, pp. 254–5.

2. Weissenburger designed several buildings in and around Nancy in a high Art Nouveau style. See, for example, Françoise-Thérèse Charpentier *et al.*, *Art Nouveau L'Ecole de Nancy*, pp. 226, 233–5, 239; Gérard Klopp (ed.), *Nancy 1900 Rayonnement de l'Art Nouveau*, 1989, pp. 132, 141, 147–8; and Christian Debrize, *Guide L'Ecole de Nancy* (La Société Nancéienne Varin-Bernier), 1989, pp. 123–5, 133 and 139.

3. For contemporary illustrations of the interior of the Café de Paris, at 41 Rue de l'Opéra, see *L'Art décoratif*, January 1989, no. 4, pp. 165–7. The café was demolished in 1955.

4. Sauvage's father formed a partnership c. 1890 with Henri Jolly. In 1898, when Henri Sauvage succeeded his father, the firm was renamed 'Entreprise Jolly Fils et H. Sauvage'.

5. Quoted in 'Un Artiste, l'œuvre de l'architecte Henri Sauvage et l'Exposition des Arts Décoratifs', *L'Organe national*, 1925, no. 5, p. 47. For further information on Sauvage's career as an architect, see *Henri Sauvage 1873–1932*, exhibition catalogue (Archives d'Architecture Moderne, Brussels), 1978.

6. For another contemporary review of the Villa Majorelle, see Louis-Charles Boileau, 'Villa rue Palissot à Nancy', *L'Architecture*, 1901, no. 40, pp. 343–7.

7. See 'L'Architecture aux Salons de 1902', *Art et décoration*, 1902, vol. 1, pp. 189–92; and 'La Villa Majorelle à Nancy', *L'Art décoratif*, August 1902, pp. 202–8 (also published in *La Lorraine artiste*, 1902, pp. 242–50).

8. The identity of the designer-decorator of the decorative frieze in the villa's dining room remains unclear. It is credited in recent literature published in Nancy to Victor Prouvé and to Henri Sauvage, while an entry in a 1903 Salon catalogue in Paris lists the design of the decorative murals in the dining room, entitled 'La Basse-Cour' and 'Enfants aux Pommes', as by Francis Jourdain and Edouard Cousin.

9. The postal address for the C.A.U.E. de Meurthe-et-Moselle is: Villa Majorelle, 1 rue Majorelle, 54000 Nancy. The office provides visitors with a selection of brochures on the villa's history. For the most comprehensive account of the villa, however, see the portfolio by Roselyne Bouvier (with an introduction by Françoise-Thérèse Charpentier), *La Villa Majorelle*; this is available through the Musée de l'Ecole de Nancy and the Musée des Beaux-Arts in Nancy.

5. *Metalware*

1. Contemporary art magazines published numerous illustrations of the desk and bookcase. See, for example, Théodore Lambert, *Meubles de style moderne Exposition Universelle de 1900* (Paris, n.d.), pl. 1, no. 1, and pl. 3, no. 4; and G.M. Jacques, 'Le Meuble français à l'Exposition', *L'Art décoratif*, July 1900, pp. 142, 143. The great success of the water-lily mounts led Majorelle to have them reproduced in small ceramic editions by Keller et Guérin of Lunéville, as bowls and containers for trinkets.

2. Octave Gerdeil, 'Les Meubles de Majorelle', *L'Art décoratif*, October 1901, p. 25.

3. Françoise-Thérèse Charpentier, in her article on the Ecole de Nancy in *Médecine de France* (cf. Chapter 3, note 20), illustrated the desk *aux nénuphars* in the collection of the Musée de l'Ecole de Nancy; the caption noted that this was a revised version, introduced in 1902, of the model shown at the 1900 Exposition Universelle. The principal difference between the two models is in the placement of the row of three short drawers and the open shelf in the desk's gallery: in the 1900 version, the three drawers were placed beneath the open shelf; in the 1902 model, the drawers were placed above the shelf. Similar modifications were introduced by Majorelle, from time to time, in other models, including the *orchidées* series.

4. The orchid-decorated ensemble for a study and its *pièce de résistance* – the imposing desk in amaranth with twin corolla lampshades – were illustrated intermittently over a period of at least five years: see, for example, *La Revue lorraine illustrée*, 1906, unpaginated colour plate; *Art et industrie*, July–December 1909, unpaginated; *L'Art décoratif aux Expositions des Beaux-Arts 1910*, pl. 5.

5. For an example of the collaboration between Robert and Prouvé, see the double entrance door illustrated in Françoise-Thérèse Charpentier's article in *Médecine de France* (see note 3 above), p. 32. For another example, a grille, see *La Décoration ancienne et moderne*, vol. 13, 1905, Paris, pl. 33.

6. *La Lorraine artiste*, 1899, p. 33.

7. For illustrations of Majorelle's architectural wrought-iron elements seen *in situ*, see Françoise-Thérèse Charpentier *et al.*, *Art Nouveau L'Ecole de Nancy* (1987), pp. 242, 244–5.

8. Majorelle incorporated these flora and plants in his designs for wrought-iron gates, balustrades, staircases, light-fixtures, etc. See Emile Nicolas, 'Les Fers forgés de M. Louis Majorelle', *La Revue lorraine illustrée*, no. 2, 1914, pp. 73–80. See also L.W., 'Un Ouvrage de ferronerie', *Le Bulletin des sociétés artistiques de l'Est*, 9ème année, no. 10, October 1903, pp. 174–5.

9. In 1922 the critic for *Mobilier et décoration*, writing in the January–February issue, p. 10, made a brief reference to the new selection of Daum glass vases, with wrought-iron mounts, introduced by Majorelle at the Salons.

10. The 'Pavillon de Marsan' bookcase and a selection of those pieces of 'Les Algues' and 'La Vigne' furniture which incorporated wrought-iron mounts are illustrated in the Contemporary Documents section, pp. 161ff.

6. *Lighting*

1. For an example of a table-lamp combining a Daum shade and a base by Cayette, see Claude Pétry, *Daum dans les Musées de Nancy*, La Société Nancéienne Varin-Bernier, 1989(?), p. 175, no. 49. Aimé Morot, another local metalworker, likewise produced wrought-iron mounts for lamps designed by Jacques Gruber.

2. Majorelle appears to have placed special emphasis on his new lamp models in four exhibitions: the 1902 and 1903 Salons of the Société des Artistes Français; the Ecole de Nancy exposition at the Pavillon de Marsan, Paris, 1903; and the Ecole de Nancy's exposition in 1904 in Nancy. Most of his most important lamps were included in his displays at these four venues, including the umbel, thistle, arrowhead, water-lily, magnolia, cactus, and orchid models.

3. *La Revue lorraine illustrée*, vol. 3, 1908, p. 33.

4. For illustrations of four of these, see *Le Bulletin artistique de l'Est*, April 1921, unpaginated colour supplement.

7. *World War I and later years*

1. See postcard: 'Les Bombardements de Nancy du 4 Septembre 1914 au 31 Octobre 1918', M. Boudrie, 60 Avenue de la Garenne, Nancy, undated; and 'Les Bombardements de Nancy, Statistique complète avec points de chute des bombes et des obus tombés sur Nancy . . .', *L'Est républicain*, 14 February 1919, p. 2, col. 3.

2. For information on the bombing of the Magasins Réunis, see *L'Etoile de l'Est*, 17 January 1916; for the death of Jean Daum, see *L'Est républicain*, 12 April 1916.

3. See, for example, *L'Est républicain*, 23 November 1916, p. 1, col. 4; *L'Eclair de l'Est*, 23 November 1916, p. 2, col. 2; *Journal de la Meurthe et des Vosges*, 22 November 1916, p. 2, col. 2, and 23 November 1916, p. 2, col. 2; and *L'Etoile de l'Est*, 26 November 1916, p. 2, col. 3.

4. Quoted in *Pages de guerre*, edited by Emile Badel, vol. 5, 1917–1918, pp. 6020–1.

5. See *L'Eclair de l'Est*, 17 October 1917.

6. Jules Majorelle *et al.*, *Louis Majorelle* (op. cit.), p. 7.

7. Alfred Lévy, 'Louis Majorelle: artiste décorateur, maître ébéniste, Nancy, 1859–1926', *Prestige*, Nancy, no. 6, 1959, p. 3.

8. *Ibid.*

9. Emile Bayard, *Le Style moderne* (1919), pp. 256ff., quoted in 'Le Fonds Ancien sur l'Art Nouveau', file in the Municipal Library, Nancy (cf. Introduction, note 2).

10. Sedeyn: as quoted in Jules Majorelle *et al.*, *Louis Majorelle* (op. cit.), p. 4.

11. Pierre Olmer, *Le Mobilier français d'aujourd'hui (1910–1925)* (Paris, 1926), p. 27.

12. Gaston Varenne, 'L'Art urbain et le mobilier au Salon d'Automne', *Art et décoration*, December 1923, p. 74.

13. Quoted by Emile Nicolas in 'Louis Majorelle', *Bulletin artistique de l'Est*, March 1926, no. 1, p. 3.

14. See E.T., 'La Rétrospective Majorelle', *L'Art vivant*, June 1926, pp. 456–7.

15 Yvanhoë Rambosson, 'Majorelle', *Mobilier et décoration*, 1933, pp. 284–93.

16. Gaston Derys, 'Quelques Ensembles des Ateliers Majorelle', *Mobilier et décoration*, 1936, pp. 409ff.

17. Emile Nicolas, 'Majorelle', *Le Pays lorrain*, no. 29, 1937, pp. 361–76.

Bibliography

Books

AMAYA, Mario, *Art Nouveau*, London and New York, 1966.

AUGUIN, Edgard, *Impressions et Souvenirs: 1875 Exposition de Nancy*, Nancy, 1875

BATTERSBY, Martin, *The World of Art Nouveau*, London, 1968

BAYARD, E., *Le style moderne*, Paris, 1919

BLOCH DERMANT, J., *L'Art du verre en France: 1860–1914*, Paris, 1975

BOUVIER, Roselyne, *La Villa Majorelle* (Editions des Amis du Musée de l'Ecole de Nancy et de la S.N.V.B.), Nancy, n.d.

BUFFET-CHALLIÉ, L., *Le Modern Style*, Paris, 1975

CHAMPIER, V., *Les Industries d'art à l'Exposition Universelle de 1900*, Paris, 1901

CHAMPIGNEULLE, Bernard, *L'Art Nouveau*, Paris, 1972

CHARPENTIER, Françoise-Thérèse *et al.*, *Art Nouveau L'Ecole de Nancy*, Paris, 1987;

—, 'L'Ecole de Nancy', in *Encylopédie illustrée de la Lorraine*, Nancy, 1987, pp. 244–314;

—, *Le Musée de l'Ecole de Nancy*, Nancy, 1982

DINGELSTEDT, K., *Le Modern Style dans les arts appliqués*, Paris, 1959

DUNCAN, Alastair, *Art Deco Furniture*, London and New York, 1984;

—, *Art Nouveau and Art Deco Lighting*, London and New York, 1978;

—, *Art Nouveau Furniture*, London and New York, 1982

GARNER, Philippe (ed.), *The Encylopedia of Decorative Arts*, London, 1978

HARRIS, Nathaniel, *Art Nouveau*, New York, 1985

JULLIAN, Philippe, *Paris Exhibition 1900, The Triumph of Art Nouveau*, London, 1975.

KLOPP, Gérard (ed.), *Nancy 1900. Rayonnement de l'Art Nouveau*, Thionville, 1989.

LAMBERT, Théodore, *Meubles et ameublements de style moderne*, Paris, 1905–6

MADSEN, Stephen Tschudi, *Sources of Art Nouveau*, Oslo, 1916

MAJORELLE, Jules, *et al.*, *Louis Majorelle*, Nancy, 1927

MARCILHAC, Félix, *La Vie et l'œuvre de Jacques Majorelle*, Paris, 1988

NICOLAS, Emile, *L'Art décoratif lorrain et l'Ecole de Nancy*, Nancy, 1917

OLMER, Pierre, *Le Mobilier français d'aujourd'hui (1910–1925)*, Paris, 1926

PROUVÉ, M., *Victor Prouvé*, Nancy, 1958

RHEIMS, Maurice, *L'Art 1900*, Paris, 1965

SCHIFF, M., *Musée de Nancy: Tableaux, dessins, statues, objets d'art, Catalogue descriptif et annoté*, Nancy, 1909

Periodicals (general)

L'Art décoratif, 1899–1916
L'Art en Lorraine, 1901–04
Art et décoration, 1898–1914
Art et industrie, 1909–11
L'Art vivant, 1925–26
Le Bulletin des sociétés artistiques de l'Est,
  1901–05, 1925–26
La Lorraine artiste, 1899–1904
Meubles et décors, 1966
Le Pays lorrain, 1937
La Revue des arts décoratifs, 1900–07
La Revue lorraine illustrée, 1901–06, 1914

Articles in periodicals

A. *Under title of article*

'The Art Nouveau Furniture of Gallé and
  Majorelle', *American Art & Antiques*,
  October 1979, pp. 86–93
'Exposition de l'Ecole de Nancy, Pavillon de
  Marsan, 1903', *The Studio*, vol. XXXV,
  1905
'Louis Majorelle', *Connaissance des arts*, no.
  195, 1968, pp. 108–9
'Majorelle', *Le Pays lorrain*, no. 29, 1937, pp.
  361–76
'Majorelle et Gallé: Maîtres du mobilier Art
  Nouveau', *L'Estampille*, February 1978, pp.
  10–17
'La Rétrospective Majorelle au Salon des
  artistes décorateurs', *L'Art vivant*, 15 June
  1926, no. 36, p. 457

B. *Under name of author*

AVRIL, R. d', 'L'Art provincial, avantages que
  la province peut offrir à l'artiste en tant que
  milieu artistique', *La Lorraine artiste*, no.
  19, 20, 1902, unpaginated
BADEL, E., 'L'Exposition des arts décoratifs à
  Nancy', *L'Immeuble et la construction dans
  l'Est*, November 1904
BELVILLE, Eugène, 'Artisans du métal. A
  propos de l'exposition du Musée Galliéra',
  L'Art décoratif, July 1905, pp. 17–23;
—, 'Daum, Lachenal, Majorelle à la galerie
  Georges-Petit', *L'Art décoratif*, VI, no. 64,
  January 1904, pp. 33–40
BOUR, E., 'Exposition lorraine d'art décoratif,
  30 octobre–4 décembre', *Bulletin des sociétés
  artistiques de l'Est*, October 1904,
  unpaginated

BRUNHAMMER, Yvonne, and RICOUR, M., 'Le
  style 1900', *Jardin des arts*, August 1958, pp.
  653–5
CHAMPIGNEULLE, Bernard, 'Meubles en quête
  d'un style', *L'Amour de l'art*, 1935, vol.
  XVI, pp. 319–24
CHARPENTIER, Françoise-Thérèse, 'L'Ecole de
  Nancy et le renouveau de l'art décoratif en
  France', *Médecine de France*, July 1964, no.
  154, pp. 17–32;
—, 'Musée des Arts décoratifs de Nancy dit de
  l'Ecole de Nancy, Nouvelles acquisitions',
  La Revue du Louvre et des Musées de France,
  no. 6, 1968, pp. 385, 392
DELACROIX, M. Ch., 'Le mobilier Majorelle ou
  l'œuvre créatrice d'un ébéniste de métier',
  L'Estampille, September 1978, pp. 19–23
DERYS, Gaston, 'Quelques Ensembles des
  Ateliers Majorelle', *Mobilier et décoration*,
  1936, pp. 409–24
DUNCAN, Alastair, 'Majorelle, Gallé, and
  Guimard. Masters of Exuberance', *The
  Australian Antique Collector*, 37th edition,
  January–June, 1989, pp. 38–42
DURET-ROBERT, François, 'Art 1900: L'Ecole
  de Nancy': 1. Meubles et sièges',
  Encyclopédie Connaissance des Arts,
  September 1970, unpaginated
EINVAUX, Roger C. d', 'L'Exposition d'art
  décoratif lorrain à Nancy', *L'Art décoratif*,
  VII, no. 77, 1905, pp. 97–164
GERDEIL, Octave, 'Les Meubles de Majorelle',
  L'Art décoratif, IV, no. 3, October 1901, pp.
  16–25
HOFMANN, M.D., 'Emile Gallé und Louis
  Majorelle, unbekannte Arbeiten und
  stilistische Bemerkungen, ein Beitrag zur
  Ecole de Nancy', *Kunst Hessen Mittelrhein*,
  8, 1968
ISSY, Edouard, 'Majorelle le maître des
  Nénuphars', *L'Estampille*, July/August
  1969, pp. 32–6
JANNEAU, G., 'L'art nouveau Bing', *Meubles et
  décors*, February 1966
JOURDAIN, Frantz, 'La Villa Majorelle à
  Nancy', *L'Art décoratif*, IV, August 1902,
  pp. 202–8; also in *La Lorraine artiste*, 1902,
  pp. 242–50
LÉVY, Alfred, 'Louis Majorelle: artiste
  décorateur, maître ébéniste, Nancy, 1859–
  1926', *Prestige*, Nancy, no. 6, 1959, pp. 2–3
NICOLAS, Emile, 'Les meubles de la Maison
  Majorelle', *La Lorraine artiste*, no. 4, 1901;

—, 'L'Ecole de Nancy', *La Revue lorraine
  illustrée*, 1908;
—, 'Les arts décoratifs à l'Exposition de
  Nancy', *Art et industrie*, October 1909, pp.
  55–9;
—, 'Les fers forgés de M. Louis Majorelle', *La
  Revue lorraine illustrée*, no. 2, 1914, pp.
  73–80;
—, 'Louis Majorelle', *Bulletin des sociétés
  artistiques de l'Est*, March 1926, pp. 1–5
RAIS, Jules, 'L'Ecole de Nancy et son
  exposition au musée des Arts décoratifs', *Art
  et décoration*, VII, April 1903, pp. 129–38
RAMBOSSON, Yvanhoë, 'Majorelle', *Mobilier et
  décoration*, 1933, pp. 284–93
SEDEYN, Emile, 'Le Meuble aux Salons', *L'Art
  décoratif*, no. 7, January–June 1905, pp.
  255–64
SOULIER, Gustave, 'Les Arts de l'ameublement
  aux Salons', *Art et décoration*, July 1898, pp.
  10–21
VIAUX, J., 'Louis Majorelle', *Revue de
  l'ameublement*, April 1964: Majorelle sales
  catalogues (undated)

Exhibition catalogues

*Exposition de l'Alliance Provinciale des
  Industries d'Art, l'Ecole de Nancy*, Union
  Centrale des Arts Décoratifs, Paris, March
  1903
L'Exposition d'art décoratif, Ecole de Nancy,
  Salle Poirel, Nancy, 1904, nos. 190–213
Exposition d'Art Décoratif de l'Ecole de Nancy,
  Société des Amis des Arts de Strasbourg,
  Palais de Rohan, 7 March–26 April 1908,
  nos. 150–55
Exposition d'Art Décoratif et Industriel Lorrain,
  Salle Poirel, Nancy, June–July 1894
  (Berger-Levrault)
L'Exposition de l'Ecole de Nancy à Paris,
  Armand Guermet (Librairie d'Art
  Décoratif), Paris, 1903
Lambert, Théodore, *Meubles de Style Moderne
  Exposition Universelle de 1900*, Charles
  Schmid, Paris, n.d.
Salon d'Automne, 1924–6
Salon de la Société des Artistes Décorateurs, 1904,
  1913–14
Salon de la Société des Artistes Français, 1902–
  03, 1907, 1912
Salon de la Société Nationale des Beaux-Arts,
  1904

Index

223